Also by John Polkinghorne and published by SPCK:

One World (1986)
Science and Creation (1988)

Published by Triangle:

The Way the World Is (1983)

SCIENCE AND PROVIDENCE

God's Interaction with the World

John Polkinghorne

First published in Great Britain 1989
SPCK
Holy Trinity Church
Marylebone Road
London NW1 4DU

Second impression 1990

Copyright © John Polkinghorne 1989

The Scripture quotations in this publication are from the
Revised Standard Version of the Bible, copyrighted 1946,
1952, © 1971, 1973 by the Division of Christian Education
of the National Council of the Churches of Christ in the
USA, and are used by permission.

British Library Cataloguing in Publication Data

Polkinghorne, J.C. (John Charlton), *1930–*
    Science and providence.
    1. Christian doctrine, related to science
    I. Title
    261.5'5

    ISBN 0-281-04398-1

Photoset, printed and bound in Great Britain by
WBC Print Ltd., Bridgend

*To the
Master, Fellows
and Scholars of
Trinity Hall,
Cambridge*

A man's mind plans his way,
   but the Lord directs his steps.

Proverbs 16.9

Alleluia; for the Lord God omnipotent reigneth.
Revelation 19.6 (AV)

CONTENTS

ACKNOWLEDGEMENTS

Some of the material of Chapters 1 and 2 was contained in my Freemantle Lecture at Balliol College, Oxford, in 1987. I am grateful to the Master and Fellows for their kind invitation to give the Lecture and for the hospitality extended to me on its occasion.

I am grateful to the Reverend John Puddefoot for some helpful suggestions, to my wife Ruth for help in correcting the proofs, and to the editorial staff of SPCK for their work in preparing the manuscript for press.

John Polkinghorne
Trinity Hall, Cambridge
September 1988

INTRODUCTION

This is the third volume of a trilogy concerned with questions arising at the interface between science and theology. The first volume (*One World*) surveyed the scene. The second (*Science and Creation*) dealt mainly with the impact upon the doctine of creation of twentieth-century discoveries about the universe and its history, and also had something to say about natural theology. Both were necessarily concerned with the generalities of physical process. In consequence the God of whom they spoke could as well have been the God of deism as the God of Christianity. The latter differs from the former in his personal and particular concern for the unfolding histories of his creatures. Though above all he is to be encountered in the individual disclosures which Scripture records and to which the Church testifies – for he is the God of Abraham, Isaac and Jacob; the God and Father of our Lord Jesus Christ – he is also a God believed to be in continual interaction with all his creation. He is to be addressed in prayer, for he exercises a providential care. The purpose of this book is to consider whether such a personal, interacting, God is a credible concept in this scientific age.

It would not be so if we lived in a universe which was merely mechanical. If the future were a rigorous consequence of the past, simply the making explicit of what was already inexorably implicit, then the best that theology could manage with intellectual integrity would be the God of deism, who had set it all a-spinning with carefully calculated care. In fact, of course, we have always known that we do not live in such a clockwork universe, for we know, as surely as we know anything, that we are not ourselves automata. If we have a certain room for manoeuvre in the way things are, it would not be altogether surprising if God, who is the sustainer of the way things are, had left for himself some such opportunity also. Advances in our scientific understanding of the world's process have now enabled us to go beyond the simple

1

assertion of the inadequacy of mere mechanism. We begin to discern the origins of our experience of open process. We are no longer scientifically condemned to a universe of frozen being, but we can start to describe a universe endowed with becoming. There is genuine novelty possible in cosmic process, and consequently genuine freedom for ourselves, and for God, is not ruled out.

This twentieth-century demise of the nineteenth-century mechanical view is due to two insights of modern physics. One is quantum theory, which revealed the apparently reliable world of everyday to be fitful and probabilistic at its constituent roots. The other insight – more important for our present purpose because it deals with phenomena at levels which are significant for events in the everyday world – is the realization that the predictable systems, studied by Newton and his successors, are exceptional in their simplicity. Once we consider complex dynamical systems, they exhibit a delicate sensitivity to circumstance which makes them intrinsically unpredictable. The future is no longer contained in the past; there is scope for real becoming. Extended to 'super-systems' like ourselves (or cosmic process) this insight offers the prospect of describing a world in which we (and God) have freedom to act. I have previously suggested (Chapter 5 of *Science and Creation*) that this resulting flexibility opens up the possibility of a complementary metaphysic in which the mental and the material are related as poles of the world-stuff in varying degrees of indeterminate/determinate organization.

These ideas are set out in Chapters 1 and 2. In the course of the discussion I suggest that the modern scientific world-view in no way makes incoherent the possibility of God's providential action within his creation. The location of his action in the flexibility of process makes it clear why it is conceivable to pray for healing, or even perhaps for rain, but inconceivable to pray for the sun to stand still or for winter to become summer. In the course of the argument I deny that we are limited solely to Wiles's deistic view of God's action as the single act of creatorly letting-be. I also reject any degree of divine embodiment as the manner of God's relation to the world.

Within the picture thus established, one can go on to consider the nature of divine providence and some of the perplexities about it (Chapter 3). If God's relation to his creation is always consistent, then

2

miracle will be an unexpected providence, made possible by an unprecedented regime, rather than a divine *tour de force* (Chapter 4). The moral and physical evils of the world result from the freedom granted by God to humankind, and to the whole developing physical process, respectively. Theodicy's free will defence, relating to moral evil, needs augmentation by a free-process defence, relating to physical evil (Chapter 5). Prayer is to be understood as the aligning of our wills with God's (the reinforcing association of our freedom for manoeuvre within cosmic process with his freedom) and the assignment of value (Chapter 6). The God who interacts with the history of the universe must be a dipolar God, possessing a temporal pole as well as an eternal pole (Chapter 7). The consequences of that for the incarnation, and the necessity from our point of view of considering sacrament as the total action of the gathered Christian community with its gifts, are briefly explored in Chapter 8. Lastly, the Final Anthropic Principle, with its attempt at a 'physical eschatology', is shown to be an inadequate basis for hope. Real hope can reside only with God, both within history and beyond it (Chapter 9).

1

The Problem

Recent years have seen a resurgence among scientists of the thought that those who seek the deepest attainable understanding of the world will have to reckon with the possibility that it will be found in theism. The beautiful structure of the laws of physics – simple, yet subtle – together with the delicate balance of their operation, by which the world's process is made fruitful, have seemed to many to speak of an Intelligence behind the unfolding evolution of the universe.[1]

Such thoughts might be expected to give encouragement to Christian believers. Yet it is possible that they are being offered a gift by the Greeks, as much to be feared as to be welcomed. For the God so discerned seems but an austere and impersonal deity; the ground of a cosmic process which rolls on without obvious concern for the fate of individuals. He commands our intellectual respect but not our love; we can wonder at his works but we are not moved to trust him in our personal lives. He is the God whom Einstein acknowledged. In reply to one of the many inquiries about his religious beliefs he wrote: 'If something is in me which can be called religious then it is the unbounded admiration for the structure of the world as far as our science can reveal it.' But he had prefixed this by saying, 'I do not believe in a personal God'.[2] The offering of a revived natural theology would have proved to be a Trojan horse for Christianity if it replaced the God and Father of our Lord Jesus Christ by the Great Mathematician.

It is, of course, clear that natural theology by itself could never lead us to the Christian God. It is a limited kind of investigation, based on certain general ideas about the pattern and structure of the world, and so it is only capable of affording limited insight. The critical question is whether that insight is such that it is capable of being reconciled with the Christian's belief in a personal and caring God, addressed in prayer and active in his providential government of the world. The new physics may encourage belief in some sort of deity, but will he prove to

4

be just a deistic Absentee Landlord? Will the very laws of nature, thought in their rational beauty to testify to his existence, so prescribe cosmic history that God is left with no room for activity within it? The inert guarantor of physical process is far from being the living God of Abraham, Isaac and Jacob. Kasper says, 'The God who no longer plays an active role in the world is in the final analysis a dead God.'[3]

The advance of science certainly seems to have had the effect in the common mind of diminishing our expectations of God's action. It was natural for ancient people to see drought as God's punishment and refreshing rain as his reward.[4] As recently as the 1928 revision of the Book of Common Prayer it was considered appropriate to include a prayer 'for seasonable weather', but when the Alternative Service Book was produced in 1980 the nearest it could come to this was a retrospective harvest collect expressing hearty thanks 'for your fatherly goodness and care in giving us the fruits of the earth in their season'. It might be thought that there is some confusion in being thankful afterwards for what we have not had the confidence to ask for beforehand. If the weather is just the outworking of the gigantic heat engine of the Earth's seas and atmosphere, then it rolls on its way, without either openness to prior pleading or the necessity for subsequent gratitude. Yet there is this deeply felt religious need to give thanks. Is that just an atavistic regression, or could it be an important insight, not yet entirely lost, that God is indeed at work in the world, our scientifically conditioned lack of expectation notwithstanding?

There is a temptingly simple answer to this question. It is to assert that God is active in the world as its Creator and Sustainer but his action is limited to that great single Act which caused and keeps in being the universe. Maurice Wiles espouses this view when he writes that 'we can make best sense of this whole complex of experience and ideas if we think of the whole continuing creation of the world as God's one act, an act in which he allows radical freedom to his human creation'.[5] The world is the way it is in its basic pattern because God wills it so, but the events that take place within it just happen as the unfolding of consequence or the choice of agents. Wiles goes on to say:

The nature of such a creation, I have suggested, is incompatible with the assertion of further particular divinely initiated acts within

5

the developing history of the world. God's act, like many human acts, is complex. I have argued that particular parts of it can rightly be spoken of as specially significant aspects of the divine activity, but not as specific, identifiable, acts of God.[6]

There is certainly important truth preserved in this holistic view of God's action. In particular, it safeguards us from a false dichotomy between the 'laws of nature' (conceived of as if operating independently of divine will) and the occasional interfering acts of an interventionist God. Such a caricature has often been taken by scientists as being what a religious believer claims when he speaks of God's activity. Paul Davies says, when talking about the evolving complexity found in the universe's history, that 'Those who invoke God as an explanation of cosmic organisation usually have in mind a *supernatural* agency, acting on the world in defiance of natural laws'.[7] The picture of the divine clockmaker, from time to time interfering to adjust the hands of the steadily ticking cosmic clock, is not one that commends itself to Christian theology. God's relationship with the world must be continuing and not intermittent; it can have nothing capricious about it, but it must be characterized by the most profound consistency. In that sense – in the sense of the unriven unity of divine attitude – it must indeed be capable of being thought of as the execution of a single great Act. Those regularities discerned by science as the laws of nature are, in fact, signals of God's reliability and faithfulness, made known in his creation.

If God is not an intervener in the world's process, yet surely, if he is the Christian God, he is in continuous interaction with it. The symbols of his relationship with his creation will need to include that of an unfolding history as well as that of a timeless act. Wiles's view, swallowed whole, has all the detachment of deism. If 'the primary usage for the idea of divine action should be in relation to the world as a whole rather than in relation to particular occurrences within it'[8] then God is in danger of becoming no more than the abstract ground of possibility, an Absentee Landlord indeed, who provides the property but leaves it to the tenants to make of it what they can. If, as certainly I believe, it is the case that God 'allows radical freedom to his human creation', it is not clear why he should have denied a similar liberty to himself. If his act, 'like many human acts, is complex', then the unpacking of that complexity may involve the recognition of different levels of relationship between God and the world, expressed through different modes of interaction. It is then the task of theology to show the mutual consistency of these differing kinds of involvement and so to exhibit the underlying harmony that enables them to be spoken of as acts of the one true God. The Christian understanding of God requires that such a range of possible action be available to him, for David Brown is surely right to say that if God makes no specific response to particular individuals 'it would seem misleading to characterise what is taking place as a personal relationship at all'.[9]

Concern with this problem has had a long history. The Fathers of the Church were not unaware of it, in the terms appropriate to their own way of thinking. Maximus the Confessor[10] distinguishes three forms of will in God. One is that of acquiescence (or concession). He illustrates it by reference to an example that poses severe difficulties for us – God's permitting Satan to put Job to excruciating test in order to demonstrate his blamelessness.[11] Whatever we may make of that, there is no doubt that part of God's interaction with the world must be that of letting agents or circumstances take their course. Without that there would be no true freedom, and the gift of love in creation must be the gift of freedom, both to humankind and also to the universe itself, as it explores its own inherent potential through its evolving process.[12] Herein lies the only possible answer to the agonizing questions, Why did God allow Auschwitz? Why did he allow the Aberfan disaster? Since nothing would be unless God permitted it to be, he is party to these terrible happenings, even if he is not their specific originator and even if we must believe them to be frustrations of his loving purpose. To this degree God is involved in all that happens. John Lucas says: 'No theist would want to deny that God is omnipotent, and that he could intervene to prevent any particular event's occurring, and therefore his non-intervention is a necessary condition for each event.'[13] God's acquiescent interaction with the world raises the acute question of theodicy. Vincent Brümmer is no doubt correct up to a point when he writes 'From the fact that God could have, but did not, prevent Auschwitz, it does not necessarily follow that we must hold him responsible for Auschwitz. We could also hold Hitler and his henchmen responsible, as in fact we usually do'[14] but the matter cannot end there. The primary responsibility clearly lies with the Nazis, just as the primary responsibility for mugging an old lady lies with her assailant, but we would not think that a powerful bystander, who watched it all happen without intervening, was altogether blameless in the latter case. We shall have to return to these questions later.

The second will of God that Maximus distinguishes is his 'economy'. The Greek word *oikonomia* had the primary meaning of administration or oversight, from which its reference widened to cover a variety of orderly circumstance.[15] Maximus' example of God's economy is the story of Joseph, the way in which the events of his life led to the preservation from famine of his father and brothers, together with all Egypt. Ancient writers also use economy to refer to the regular sequence of natural phenomena. One says 'By economy, it became dusk'. In modern terms the idea would translate into the unfolding process of the world, whose regularity and stability reflect the economic will of its Creator. We might say: 'By economy the galaxies condensed; by economy replicating molecules were able to form; by economy *homo sapiens* evolved; by economy humankind is able to exercise in society mutual restraint for the common good.' God's economy is obviously related to God's acquiescence, the former being the positive side of cosmic process, in contrast to the latter's negative aspect. Concisely, one might say that economy is that for which we feel thankful in the ordinary working of the world. Acquiescence and economy lie central to Wiles's view of God's one universal Act, the given circumstance of creation.

Certainly the recognition of God's preservation of the regular order of the world must be seen to be a large and important part of his action upon it. The Hebrews rightly feared the waters of chaos, and F. R. Tennant was correct when he said that Christian theism 'must be sufficiently tinged with deism to recognize a relatively settled order'.[16] Indeed people have thought that the Christian expectation of an orderly but contingent cosmos was an important ideological prerequisite for the development of modern science.[17] Yet order must not congeal into rigidity; the restraint of God's general reliability must not result in his total impotence with respect to individual occurrences. The outdated mechanical universe of pre-twentieth century physical science would not have been the fitting creation of the Christian God, though

8

it could certainly be said to exhibit his economy and acquiescence. It will not do to confine God's interaction with the world to a deistic maintenance of the total process. So Maximus goes on to speak of a third will of God, that of purpose (*eudokia*, good pleasure). His illustration is the call of Abraham. Here the example chosen is one that is, perhaps, easy for us to accept. We have learnt about levels in our psyches lying deeper than that of the rational ego of everyday awareness. Modern depth psychology, particularly that following the insights of Jung, seeks to map this interior territory, finding it populated by powerful and symbolic psychic forces. If there is a God, the ground of being, it does not seem inconceivable that he might find in this archetypal world of the unconscious his point of individual interaction with us. Christopher Bryant testifies how Jung's idea of the Self as the fundamental integrating archetype, active in the depths of the psyche, helped him to identify the action of God in part of his experience:

> It was Jung's idea of the self, the whole personality, acting as a constant influence on my conscious aims and intentions in a manner I was powerless to prevent, that brought home to me the inescapable reality of God's rule over my life. So long as I thought of God's providence as an abstract truth, part of theistic belief, it made no powerful impact on me. But it was quite another matter if God's guiding hand was within my own being, within the fluctuations of mood and the ups and downs of health.[18]

Not all will agree with Jungian ideas, but the mysterious complexity of human personality does seem open to such divine influence. Does that exhaust the possibilities for God's particular interaction with his creation? When we pray, should we restrict ourselves to requests relating to attitudes (Lord, give me courage) and eschew requests relating to circumstance (Lord, heal my illness)? Even to state the question is to begin to be uneasy about a minimalist answer to it. The increasing recognition of the psychosomatic element in medicine, indicates that there are connections between mental attitude and physical circumstance. If our thoughts can affect our bodies, why should God be believed to be restricted to influence within the psyche alone? Indeed, if man is a psychosomatic unity, as I think there is good reason to think that he is, is there any *sense* in postulating such a restriction? Exactly how brain and mind are related is beyond our present power to say, but that they are related is clear from the effects of drugs and brain damage. If all mental processes have brain correlates, and that is true of the operation of the unconscious mind as well as that of the conscious ego, then God could not interact with the depths of our psyches without also interacting in some way with the material processes of our brains. If that is the case, one can then go on to inquire about the possibility of his interacting in a specific way with matter not organized into complex wholes supporting consciousness. In plain words, we seem to have opened up for us the possibility of those particular acts of God which are traditionally called providence and, even, miracle. We shall defer to later chapters the discussion of these questions and of the difficulties related to their answer. For the moment, let me say that I agree with Peter Baelz when he says: 'If the scientific view of the order of the world can make room for human freedom and human volition without disrupting its own procedures, so too it can make room for divine freedom and divine volition.'[19] And I would want to go on to say that if the scientific view of the world cannot accommodate human freedom and human volition, so much the worse for it, for it would then be manifestly inadequate to describe the way things are.[20] (Of course, I am aware of the philosophical debate about human freedom, but for me it is a fundamental fact about experience. Deny it, and the very act of denial becomes the empty mouthing of an automaton. Ultimately the denial of human freedom is incoherent.)

These considerations motivate us to seek an understanding of God's action in the world which goes beyond simple assertion that he is the sustainer of regular process. He is not just the abstract God of natural theology but he is also the living God, known to Israel and the Church through the works of his Spirit. He is the one who is worshipped by the elders in the Book of Revelation with the words 'We give thanks to thee, Lord God almighty, who art and wast, that thou hast taken thy great power and begun to reign.'[21] The question remains, how can this be?

Fideist and existentialist alike decline to attempt an answer. Martin Gardner, who is interesting as being a fideist standing outside all traditional religions, says: 'I cannot understand how my will can be free. How much less can I understand how God's will can be free? . . . Nor do I worry about such questions. Trying to play God is too much of a strain.'[22] An existential theologian like Rudolf Bultmann equally refuses to be drawn on the matter. The essence for him is our relationship with God, not his relationship with the physical world. 'Knowledge of God as creator contains primarily knowledge of man – man, that is, in his creatureliness, and in his situation of being one to whom God has laid claim.'[23] Bultmann's programme of demythologization hands over the exterior world to science and the interior world to religion. If there are connections between these two worlds, then they are unknown and unknowable. Yet, if we take the psychosomatic unity of humankind seriously, as the successes of modern biology certainly encourage us to do,[24] the exterior/interior division is, in the end, untenable. And if we take the unity of knowledge seriously, then we must at least make the attempt to integrate the scientific and theological pictures of the world, however much the apophatic avowals of the fideist and the existentialist may warn us to be modest about our expectations of success.

A theologian who is often claimed to have made an important contribution to our understanding of these matters is Austin Farrer. That might seem surprising, since in some ways Farrer's stance approximates to that of the existentialist. He tells us that: 'We are concerned with [God's] purpose and activity solely as an operation to which we commit ourselves . . . the causal joint (could there be said to be one) between God's action and ours is of no concern in the activity of religion.' What we have to do is to 'embrace the divine will'.[25] Nevertheless, Farrer stands in a tradition of theological thought which has not despaired of articulating what it is talking about, so that he does in fact go on to discuss the 'causal joint', in terms of his celebrated notion of 'double agency'. However, it proves to be an elusive concept:

> We believe that God's way of acting is the infinitely higher analogue of our way, but we cannot conceive it otherwise than in terms of our own. God's agency must actually be such as to work omnipotently on, in or through creaturely agencies without forcing them or competing with them. But as soon as we try to conceive it as action,

11

we degrade it to the creaturely level and place it in the field of interacting causalities. The result can only be (if we take it literally) monstrosity and confusion.[26]

If that is so, it is not clear what progress we are supposed to have made, particularly as, even in its obscurity, the discussion seems framed solely in terms of God's interaction with agents and not with the whole of his creation. No doubt Farrer is right to say that 'every theologian is bound to find a course between anthropomorphism and ineffability',[27] but he seems to have ended up on the darker side of that pathway.

A favourite analogy – used by Farrer himself – to which to turn for help has been that of characters in a novel written by a creative author, which depend upon him but which are often said to develop a life of their own as the story unfolds. Certainly a responsible author is constrained by his perception of the personalities of those about whom he is writing, but he retains extraordinary and arbitrary powers to order the circumstances of their lives. Charlotte Brontë can decree, in her authorial providence, that the distraught and wandering Jane Eyre shall end up at the cottage of those who, unknown to her, are her distant relatives and through whom she will learn of a timely inheritance. That is the exercise of a naked power of disposal which seems to bear little analogy to the subtle relationships of God to a world to which he has given a large measure of creaturely freedom. If we thought it as unproblematic that God could thus fix the outcome of events, as we believe it to be unproblematic that an author has control over the arrangements of his plot, we should not write so many books about God's action in the world.

John Lucas has recourse to a different picture. He says: 'we speak of Solomon's having built the Temple, though it is doubtful whether with his own hands he so much as placed one stone upon another'.[28] In other words, Lucas's picture of double agency is that of the co-operative interaction of agents. The causal joint in the construction of the Temple is then manifest. Solomon told the masons to do it. This analogue will only help us in our understanding of God's action in the world if we embrace the exercise of his purposeful will, as when he called Abraham. So we return to the question of how widely that third type of will can find its expression in the process of the world.

Farrer, who sometimes in his writings exhibits something of the metaphysician's disdain for the pedestrian details of physics, nevertheless felt that the modern identification of matter and energy somehow helped, for 'If God creates energies he creates activities'.[29] Farrer thought that this insight removed the buffer of created object between divine will and created becoming. Now it is certainly the case that the modern picture of matter is dynamic rather than static in character, but the equation $E = mc^2$ as much asserts the material property of energy as it asserts the energetic property of matter. Inertia is thereby confirmed rather than abolished. It seems to me to illustrate the dangers of being deceived by verbal allusion, imperfectly understood, to feel that in *this* respect modern physics offers greater openness of the world to divine action than did its Newtonian predecessor. However, it is a major concern of this essay to suggest that in other respects the modern understanding of the nature of physical process is indeed helpful in the consideration of God's possible action in the world. I shall suggest that recent advances in science point to an openness and flexibility within physical process – not only at the microscopic level of quantum theory but also at the macroscopic level of large systems – which begins to offer hope of some understanding of how both we ourselves, and also God, can exercise our wills in the physical world. Maurice Wiles felt that the 'already problematic character' of attempts to discern God's specific activity have been increased by 'our fuller understanding of the ordered patterns of the natural world and of history. The possibility of affirming divine action is not ruled out but its specific location is still harder to detect.'[30] History has never been susceptible to neat pattern making. As far as natural science is concerned, advances in physics in this century have abolished the merely mechanical view of the universe which earlier centuries had espoused. Many detailed problems remain about the nature and location of God's activity but its general conceivability has been enhanced by recent developments in science. Neither God nor man is perceived as caught in the grip of relentless causal rigidity.

A profitable line to pursue would appear to be that of analogies between God's action and our own experience as agents. After all, the latter is the most complex and interesting experience of which we can all agree that we have direct knowledge. The attempt can take two forms. One tries to proceed from our ideas about how God may interact with us, to construct ideas about how he might interact with the rest of creation. Thus it tries to proceed by assimilating the nature of the rest of the universe to our nature. It has, therefore, tended to depend upon some form of panpsychism, attributing a rudimentary, if unconscious, mental pole to all matter. The other approach notes that, although we believe that the matter that makes up our bodies obeys the same physical laws as matter everywhere else, yet we are consciously able to exercise our will through the instrumentality of our bodies. It therefore tries to assimilate God's action in the world to our action in our bodies.

The most sustained modern articulation of the first approach is to be found in the work of the process theologians,[31] based on the philosophy of A. N. Whitehead. For Whitehead, the fundamental metaphysical category is that of event. What we think of as continuing objects are for him chains of events. Each event has both a subjective and an objective phase – the selection of a possible outcome followed by its actual realization. God's action is by way of enticement at the subjective stage, the lure (a favourite Whiteheadian word) which he exerts on persons and protons alike. Concrete reality lies with the world; God can only hope to influence its self-creative process by being the reservoir of its past experiences, the presenter of present possibility and the persuader of future development. Colin Gunton says of process theology that it 'has been described as a sophisticated form of animism',[32] so greatly does it locate initiative in panpsychic matter. The God of Whitehead is a curiously passive deity – Keith Ward calls him 'the cosmic sponge'[33] – just as Whitehead's event-based metaphysic is a curiously episodic view of reality.

Panpsychic ideas are far from persuasive. They run counter to our understanding of the physical world, admittedly become more subtle and elusive in its nature with the advent of quantum theory, but still – despite the discontinuity of wave-function collapse and the fitfulness of statistical prediction – a world exhibiting continuity through conservation laws and regularity through the Schrödinger equation.[34] The invocation of a latent psychic pole of all matter does not seem to afford any insight helpful in resolving the persisting perplexities which beset the interpretation of quantum theory. We shall see that, if there is any truth lying behind this first approach, it does not need to be expressed in the extravagant language of panpsychism.

The second of the two approaches, namely that drawing an analogy between our action in our bodies and God's action in the world, seems to many to be the better line to pursue. Arthur Peacocke says:

> I would suggest that this problem of the human sense of being an agent, of being a self, an 'I', acting in this physical causal nexus, is of the same ilk as the relation of God to the world. How can God act in a world in which every event is tied to every other by regularities which the sciences explain with increasing power and accuracy? Is it not a parallel and similar question to ask: How can I, experiencing myself mentally as an agent, initiate processes, within the causal physical nexus, that is my body, which themselves *are* my intended actions?[35]

It is clearly worth looking into, though two substantial problems are apparent from the start. One is that it is, to some extent, a flight from the unknown to the Unknown. Although we have experience of our own embodiment, we understand very little indeed of its detailed mode of application. The appeal to this analogy will, therefore, lack the full explanatory power that would result from recourse to a model whose working was open to us. The second difficulty is that, like all analogies, it will fail and this is particularly likely to happen in significantly limiting ways for all analogies applied to the God who transcends our ability to grasp. A whole-hearted embracing of this particular approach would make God the world-soul and lead to the pantheism of Spinoza or Einstein. Since our concern is with the action of the Christian God, who is far more than just the ground of cosmic process, the result would be a failure for the enterprise. A way out, suggested by some,[36] is panentheism – the idea that God includes the world but exceeds it. This affords him a direct relationship with the physical universe but prevents his being totally imprisoned by it. The problem then lies in the danger that such a view compromises the world's freedom to be itself, which God has given to his creation, and also the otherness that he retains for himself. Commenting on

15

Christian panentheism, Moltmann says: 'The elements of truth in this view are turned into their opposite once the capacity to distinguish is suppressed by the will to synthesise'.[37] There are distinctions between God and the world that Christian theology cannot afford to blur. They lie at the root of the religious claim that meeting with God involves personal encounter, not just a communing with the cosmos.

Vernon White protests against any 'way of eminence' which attempts to proceed to the divine by simple enhancement of the human. God is so much more than man-writ-cosmically-large that, in his view, such a method will insufficiently stretch the language being used. In relation to God's activity, White says 'we should insist on some distinguishing feature for divine action so that it may be truly identified as divine'.[38] The book from which that quotation is taken is subtitled 'A Concept of Special Divine Action' and it is its author's aim to argue for a belief in 'a God of the details of life, a God of the sparrows'.[39] Yet it is not clear how immediately visible the action of God can be. Because he is the ground of all, he must be compatible with all that is. He is not just a powerful agent among the agencies at work in the world, but he is the sustainer of the whole process. In principle, for physical causes we can observe their effects by contrasting the consequences of their presence with the consequences of their absence, or (if like the gravitational field they cannot wholly be eliminated) at the very least their attenuation. But we cannot perform the experiment of seeing what the universe is like when God is removed. I believe it would cease to exist, and my atheist friend thinks that nothing would be changed, but neither of us can put it to the test. This leads David Pailin to say:

> it is logically erroneous to seek empirical verification for theism or to attempt to specify situations which, if they came to be, would falsify basic theistic claims . . . the question of theism is the primary metaphysical question of whether reality as a whole is ultimately meaningful or finally absurd, and its logical status must be perceived accordingly. Empirical considerations may contribute to our decision about the truth of such claims about God's reality but they can never decisively verify or falsify them.[40]

The austerity of the first sentence is modified by the contribution admitted in the final sentence. There must be aspects of the world which tend to a theistic or atheistic view, otherwise there would be no motivation for one belief or the other and we should all sink into total agnosticism. The fact that the debate continues shows that this is not the case, though certainly neither side has knockdown argument available to it. While it will not be possible to exhibit the naked action of God, we must expect there to be occasions when belief in that action will be more persuasively suggested than on others. Even someone like Maurice Wiles, who is committed to the view of God's action as a single Creatorly fiat, can acknowledge that 'particular parts of [that act] can rightly be spoken of as significant aspects of divine activity' though he wants to deny that they are to be considered as 'specific identifiable acts of God'.[41] Without some recourse to the particular there is a danger that the God who does everything will be perceived as the God who does nothing. Yet, to the problem of God's particular activity, we must add the problem of God's particular inactivity, his apparent absence from those occasions when his powerful presence seems most needed and desired. No account of God's action can avoid the fact of the widespread existence of evil and suffering in the world, with the challenge that this presents to theodicy.

Involved in all our discussion is an inescapable dialectic tension present in all Christian talk about God: the ground of being, encountered in mystical experience and immanent in the working of the world/the sovereign Lord, encountered in personal confrontation, and the transcendent ruler of his creation; the God of general process/the God of special providence; the timeless God of the philosophers/the God of Abraham, Isaac and Jacob, caught up in the history of his people. Our view of God will have to be sufficiently rich and complex to be able to embrace these apparent contradictions, all of which arise from religious experience and reflection. It will also have to meet the challenge presented by the plain speaking of Ian Ramsey, when he said that, if the Christian claims are 'to go beyond picturesque, inspiring, stories, at least talk about God's activity must be literal and univocal, straightforwardly reliable'.[42]

This chapter has tried to survey some of the problems involved in speaking of God's action in the world. The issues it has raised will have to be explored in more detail in the chapters that follow.

2

Embodiment and Action

Our first task is to pursue further the possibility that God's action in the universe might operate in a way analogous to our action in our physical bodies. It is a notion that had occurred to Descartes. He wrote to the Cambridge platonist, Henry More, that 'the only idea I can find in my mind to represent the way in which God or an angel can move matter is the one which shows me the way in which I am conscious I can move my body by my own thought'.[1] Of course, Descartes' ideas were strongly dualistic, with a clear division between mind and matter and with the real 'I' residing on the mental side of that divide. (He wrote: 'it is certain that I am really distinct from my body and could exist without it.'[2]) The fatal weakness of his system is just the unresolved 'causal joint' by means of which the human ghost within manipulates the machine that it inhabits. Appeal to the pineal gland as the seat of the soul was a pretty desperate attempt at a remedy. In the end, Cartesianism had to fall back on occasionalism – the divinely synchronized ticking of the mental and material clocks, so that God arranges for my hand to move when I will it to move. Thus, ironically, it is only by an appeal to the direct exercise of divine action upon the world that the later Cartesians could come to terms with human activity. Instead of using our embodiment to throw light on God's action, the latter is found to be a necessary condition for understanding the former!

Descartes' remark to More was not going so far as to talk of God's embodiment, as is made clear by his reference also to an angel. Such a notion would not be at all appealing in a dualistic system, where all real initiative lies with the mind. However modern thought about man encourages us to regard ourselves as psychosomatic unities and this makes possible a reassessment of the value of the analogy of embodiment. Human bodily experience is characterized by:

1 Some power of direct action (I can move my limbs, but I cannot

directly will a change in the peristaltic rhythms of my intestines).
2 Some degree of direct awareness (I feel aches and pains but I am not directly aware of my blood pressure).
3 A limitation of perspective (I view the world from 'within' my body).
4 A vulnerability to changes in the physical circumstances of my body (if my brain tissues degenerate because of Alzheimer's disease, my personality will become demented).

Clearly, the analogues of 1 and 2, suitably stretched and enhanced by the replacement of partial power by total ability, would provide expression of divine omnipotence and omniscience in relation to the world. Equally clearly, the limitation 3 would be unacceptable for God. Richard Swinburne makes this a major ground for his criticism of embodiment ideas:

> The claim that God has no body is the denial of a more substantial embodiment [i.e. going beyond 1 and 2], and above all the denial that God controls and knows about the material universe by controlling and getting information from one part directly and controlling and getting information from other parts only by their being in causal interaction with the former part.[3]

Grace Jantzen, who is the most fluent contemporary defender of divine embodiment, has grounds for replying to this by saying: 'But this latter consideration does not, surely, count against God's having a body but in favour of it – only, his body must be understood to be the whole universe, not an individual part of it.'[4]

There remains property 4, which is for me the rock on which the idea of divine embodiment finally founders. The difficulty is not that God should in any degree be vulnerable to the world. The doctrine of divine impassibility is not intended to insulate God from his creation but to assert that 'His will is determined from within instead of being swayed from without'.[5] The God of the Jews and Christians, who suffers when his people suffer, is not a God living in splendid isolation. The act of creation involved a kenotic action by God in which he accepted the vulnerability implicit in any gift of freedom by love to the beloved.[6] If these ideas are correct, they have two implications. The true meaning of divine impassibility asserts that God is not in thrall to

19

any creature. The true meaning of divine vulnerability lies in the acceptance of the otherness of the beloved. I agree with Vanstone's description of the Christian God as *Deus non passibilis sed passus*[7] – the God who is impassible but vulnerable. Our discussion will show that one or other of those predicates would be threatened by divine embodiment.

We are in thrall to our bodies, in the sense expressed by property 4 and in the ultimate sense of the dissolution of death. It seems to me that the true Christian hope is not that of survival (the Cartesian existence without a body) but of resurrection (the reconstitution of that complex pattern of material/mental activity, which is me, in some new environment of God's choosing). If talk of divine embodiment is to make any sense, then surely radical changes in the character of the physical world must have significant consequences for the One embodied in it. The universe as we observe it today is a collection of aggregations of gravitationally-condensed matter, formed on different length scales, from galaxies through stars to planets, and composed of constituents held together by nuclear and electromagnetic forces, in systems of complexities ranging from single ions to ourselves. If we peer back fifteen billion years to within a minute fraction of a second of the primal event of the big bang, we have good reason to suppose that there was then a time when the whole universe was a highly energetic soup of quarks and gluons and other exotic particles. If we peer forward many billions of years into the future, we have reason to expect either a cosmic collapse back again into a quark soup, followed by a subsequent total collapse into the big crunch, or the decay of a still-expanding universe into low-grade radiation.[8] Would it make any sense to talk of divine embodiment and not to suppose that these extraordinary changes in the state of the physical universe would have significant impact on the God so embodied? In particular, many scientists take the view that the physical world sprang into being with the singularity of the big bang, time coming into being with it. What would that mean for an embodied God?

It is significant that Jantzen acknowledges that: 'It is true that, if the universe is the embodiment of God, then the universe taken as a whole must be everlasting.'[9] Scientifically, we are not able to plumb the past beyond the moment of the big bang, but it is, at the very least, precarious to presume a cosmic history before it. As one extrapolates back closer and closer to the big bang singularity, matter is found to be in states of higher and higher energy, more and more remote from regimes of which we have the experience to speak with justified confidence. Of course, speculation can attempt to go beyond the reach of knowledge. For example, it has been suggested that the whole big bang might be just the inflation of a primeval vacuum fluctuation.[10] Prior to that, God's body would be the vacuum – not quite as empty an entity as one might think, since the quantum vacuum is a richly structured state, but minimal nevertheless. Jantzen herself refers to suggestions of an oscillatory scenario for the universe, so that it springs forth from each successive big bang endowed with new laws of physics, only to collapse again into the cosmic melting pot of the next big crunch, before rebounding for another evolutionary cycle.[11] These daring ideas should be seen for what they are, metaphysical flights of the imagination rather than sober physical theories. Contemporary science offers no firm support for the notion of an everlasting universe. Even if the idea of cosmic oscillation were correct, combined with divine embodiment it would have the curious theological consequence of a God everlastingly engaged in ceaseless change. He would be the Cosmic Quick Change Artist. Such a God could hardly be called impassible.

An embodied God could only escape from being swept along in the changes and chances of his fleeting world by the naked exercise of his divine power. Jantzen says: 'If the universe is God's body, God's self-formation, and he is in complete control of it, then he can change it in whatever way he choses.'[12] Of course, the omnipotent God could always extricate himself from the trap of property 4, but could he do so and remain the Creator of a world given the freedom to be itself? Could he retain the vulnerability of love? It seems that divine embodiment will force God to destroy the liberty of creation if he seeks to safeguard his own independence. God and the world are so closely linked by embodiment that one must gain the mastery over the other. Either divine impassibility must triumph by the assertion of a divine tyranny over the world (an idea so detested by Whitehead), or divine vulnerability must triumph through the world's imposing itself upon God (just as Whitehead's God has to rely upon the process of the world

21

for the coming-to-be of his consequent nature). Only by breaking the tie implicit in embodiment can God be let be to be God and his creation be let be to be itself.

I do not think that this necessary degree of separation is achieved by Arthur Peacocke's 'biological model', based on the metaphor of a maternal sustaining of the foetus in the womb, so that one has 'an analogy of God creating the world within herself'.[13] (Not the least of the difficulties of this model is that the growing child is of one substance with its mother, flesh from flesh.) To the extent that they enmesh God and the world, all panentheistic theories are going to threaten the mutually free relation of God and his creation. I prefer Moltmann's account:

> it is only the assumption of a self-limitation by God himself preceding his creation which can be reconciled with God's divinity without contradiction. In order to create a world 'outside' himself, the infinite God must have made room beforehand for finitude in himself. It is only a withdrawal by God into himself that can free the space into which God can act creatively. The *nihil* for his *creatio ex nihilo* only comes into being because – and in as far as – the omnipotent and omnipresent God withdraws his presence and restricts his power.[14]

It seems to me that this understanding draws the sting from Hartshorne's criticism of classical theism, in the course of his defence of panentheism, which Gunton summarizes by saying 'If things were simply "outside" God, there would be a greater reality than God, God and the world.'[15] Since the world is only in being because of God's free making room for it, its existence in addition to God does not create a greater reality, for we are speaking ontologically and not arithmetically.

Before we leave this question of divine embodiment, we should also note another more naive difficulty. Accepting the idea would imply that the universe is really an organism. What exactly this would entail is hard to specify but it would surely have to go far beyond just a degree of mutual interaction between its parts, even if these interactions produced some homeostatic regulation of the whole. For the sort of organism appropriate to be God's body there would have to be some heightened analogue of the immense interconnectivity of the human

22

brain. James Lovelock's well-known suggestion that the Earth should be thought of as an organism (which he calls Gaia[16]) fails to be persuasive just because of that lack of appropriate degree of reflexive complexity within Earth's admittedly many and delicately balanced relationships. The universe, at its level, looks even less like an organism called Theos. I do not want at all to argue for a reductionist view of the world that sees it simply as an aggregation of elementary particles. The persisting togetherness-in-separation, which quantum mechanics implies for two elementary particles which have once interacted with each other,[17] is just one corrective to such a view. Yet, when one surveys the web of cosmic process, it seems to have a different, less intricately reciprocal, character than, say, that of the biochemical dance of even a single cell. It is hard to think of ourselves as organelles within the divine body.

This discussion has been stuttering, partly because it is so hard to say exactly what an organism is,[18] partly because it seems so unsophisticated just to blurt out 'If the universe is God's body, then what is God's nervous system?' though at root that is a severe difficulty.

Abandonment of the notion of God's corporality in this universe does not mean that we must give up any hope of gaining analogical insight into his action in the world from the consideration of our own embodiment. We shall just have to be circumspect in the way we apply the analogy. Rather than trying to press the correspondence too closely, we must be content to address the general question of how it is that there is room within the apparently regular causal network of physical process for our basic (I would want to say undeniable) experience of the exercise of the will. If we have some purchase on what happens in the world, may not God enjoy analogous room for manoeuvre?

To ask that question returns us to the issues of the previous chapter. Most of us feel that as far as we are concerned the laws of physics are a given within which we have to operate. Even in the West that is not quite a universal view. The great quantum physicist, Erwin Schrödinger, faced himself with the following two premises:

1 My body functions as a pure mechanism according to the Laws of

nature; 2 Yet I know by incontrovertible direct experience, that I am directing its motions . . .

from which he reached the astounding conclusion that

The only possible inference from these two facts is, I think, that I – I in the widest meaning of the word, that is to say every conscious mind that has ever said or felt 'I' – am the person, if any, who controls the 'motion of the atom' according to the Laws of Nature.[19]

Thus Schrödinger was led to embrace the Eastern equation of Atman and Brahman, the merging of the individual self and the Universal Self. I personally cannot follow that way. It stands in too great a contradiction to my experience of individual responsibility before the God who is Other, and my experience of distinctness from other persons and the world around me. Neither do I accept the cloudy and mysterious claim of the so-called Participatory Anthropic Principle, that the character of the universe has been affected by the operation of observers within it, a claim to my mind in no way clarified by highly dubious appeals to quantum theory.[20] The extent to which the latter – if at all – licenses the idea of an observer-created reality is very tightly circumscribed and in no way relates to fundamental law and circumstance. So I do not think that I have a hand in the laws of physics, though I certainly think that God does. Their discerned regularities are pale reflections of his faithfulness towards his creation; they are expressions of his acquiescent and economic wills. He will not interfere in their operation in a fitful or capricious way, for that would be for the Eternally Reliable to turn himself into an occasional conjurer. Yet the laws of nature do not constitute a strait-jacket restraining divine action.

Firstly, our current perception of these laws does not necessarily constitute an exhaustive description of the rationally coherent world as it actually exists. We cannot exclude the possibility that in novel circumstances, of which we have no previous direct experience, novel phenomena will occur. Physics never claims more than verisimilitude, an adequate map of regimes already explored. Entry into a new regime often reveals unexpected and unforeseeable new phenomena. Absolute and completely general truth is beyond our grasp. Secondly, those

24

laws of nature that we do know do not imply that there is no flexibility for action, both human and divine, within the process they describe. Pursuit of the first point opens up the possibility for what is usually called miracle; pursuit of the second point opens up the possibility for what is usually called providence. Because I am trying to understand God's activity within a framework of his consistently reliable relation to the world, ultimately the contrast between these two kinds of action will dissolve, proving to reside in the degree of understanding possessed by the observer, rather than a different attitude in the Actor. The miraculous is simply the providential in unusual circumstances.

God's purposive action within the flexibility of process may be expected to bear some analogy with our human experience of willed activity, for which we know that there must be such flexibility, since we exercise it all the time. How can we picture its coming about? The answer will lie in such modest understanding as we may possess of how our psychosomatic unity is realized within the physical world.

It may be true, as John Macquarrie tells us, that philosophers from Plotinus to Whitehead have pointed out that 'inert formless matter cannot evolve into such a universe as we know it',[21] but it is also true that matter, as we understand it today, is very far from being inert and formless. The insights of cosmology, evolutionary biology and molecular genetics, all bear witness to the astonishing potentiality with which matter is endowed. The austere simplicities of the laws of fundamental physics provide the basis for the coming-to-be of systems as complex and fruitful as ourselves. I agree with Arthur Peacocke when he writes that: 'We cannot avoid arriving at a new view of matter which sees it as manifesting mental, personal and spiritual activities.'[22] This does not come about by a reduction of the mental to the role of an epiphenomenon of the physical, but rather by its being the manifestation of the genuine conceptual novelty possessed by systems of matter-in-flexible-organization. François Jacob puts the relationship of life and matter neatly when he says: 'Biology can neither be reduced to physics nor do without it.'[23]

Panpsychism sensed that this was so, but it went the wrong way about understanding it. Our mental powers do not result from the aggregation of the psychic residues of the electronic and nuclear matter of our bodies, anymore than the wetness of water derives from residual moisture present in each H_2O molecule. These properties are ones that can only be perceived in the whole, for they arise from relationships only expressible in the whole.

Elsewhere I have advocated a complementary metaphysic. The idea is to regard the material and the mental as complementary poles of the world-stuff, encountered in greater or lesser states of organization and flexibility.[24] The aim is to do justice to both mind and matter as true aspects of reality, but by the notion of complementarity to avoid an unacceptable dualism dividing them. Such an invocation of quantum mechanical metaphor (compare it with the essential complementarity of wave and particle required for the description of subatomic matter) only ceases to be a slogan, and becomes of modest explanatory value, if it can point to the reconciling linkage of its dialectic poles. In plainer words, how do mind and matter relate to each other? Wave/particle duality is a coherent way of talking about electrons, not because each particle has a little bit of undulation in it which then adds up to a big wave (that would be the 'panpsychic' fallacy) but because quantum field theory shows us that states with an *indefinite* number of particles can manifest wavelike properties.[25] I have suggested that this encourages the thought that a mental pole emerges from a material pole, not by the direct analogy of an indefinite amount of matter, but by the indirect analogy of an indefinitely flexible degree of organization of the matter. I have also suggested that this complementarity enables us, as psychosomatic unities, to participate at our mental pole in a noetic world (a world of ideas) but that it is also necessary to suppose that world to have inhabitants which are not mental/material amphibians like ourselves. A simple example would be the truths of mathematics. This noetic world (which bears some relation to Moltmann's 'heaven'[26] and to Popper's 'World 3'[27]) is a created world and is not part of God, though dependent upon him. The essential notion is that humans are mind/matter amphibians, participating in both material and mental worlds but sharing both with other entities.

If these ideas have any validity, they might be helpful in thinking about God's purposive action in the world. They imply that our willed interaction with the universe arises from the presence of indefiniteness, or flexibility, within its process. For us, that indefiniteness presumably refers to the flexibility present in the actual processes of our bodies. As mental/material amphibians we are inescapably embodied. God's action would then relate to the presumably much greater flexibility present within the total flux of cosmic process. That flexibility would be the ground necessary for God's particular action, but not for his being, so that in this picture God interacts with the world but it is not proper to speak of the world as his body. *He* is no amphibian. The necessary degrees of divine and creaturely independence can be maintained. In the traditional language of the theologians of the Eastern Church, God acts in the world through his energies, not his essence.

It is next necessary to consider the origin of this indefiniteness, or open flexibility, which it is supposed makes possible the integration of the mental with the material, and permits God's purposive action in the world. An obvious candidate might have appeared to be provided by quantum phenomena. It is notorious that quantum events are believed by the majority of physicists to be constrained only by overall statistical regularity in their patterns of occurrence. Individual events are characterized by a radical randomness and are even spoken of as being 'uncaused'. It might be thought that here is to be found the necessary room for manoeuvre, both for God and for ourselves. Such a view has been proposed[28] but it has not commended itself widely. It is likely to founder on the propensity for randomness to generate regularity, for order to arise from chaos.[29] The aggregation of individually chance events at one level is liable to compose itself into a highly predictable pattern at a higher level. The practice of Life Insurance Offices is based upon this very tendency. The life expectancy of an individual client is highly uncertain, but the actuaries can be tolerably secure in their forecasts of how many people in a large sample of given age will die in the next few years. In an exactly similar way, the everyday certainties of the world of Newtonian mechanics arise from out of their fitful quantum substrate. As far as we can tell, most of the processes likely to be of significance for our action on the world (such as those involved in the neurophysiological operations of our brains) proceed at levels above those characterized by quantum mechanical uncertainty. That is why Schrödinger – who after all was not unaware of the peculiarities of quantum theory, though he did not much like them – felt able to take as one of his premises 'My body functions as a pure mechanism according to the Laws of Nature'. If exploitation of Heisenberg uncertainty is not the way in which we are able to be ourselves, it is also unlikely to be the way in which God exercises his purposive will. I am not saying that there are never circumstances in which quantum effects are amplified to have macroscopic consequences, only that they are unlikely by themselves to provide a sufficient basis for human or divine freedom, even supposing God's will and ours to be exercised in the hole-and-corner way of influencing quantum events.[30]

A much more promising line of inquiry would seem to be provided by the modern recognition of the subtlety of behaviour enjoyed by complex dynamical systems. When Schrödinger spoke of our bodies as 'pure mechanism', the picture which may well have arisen in your mind (and which may well have been present in his mind too when he wrote the phrase) might have been that of an intricate piece of machinery, regular and reliable in its working. A steadily ticking clock would be the paradigm case. From Newton almost to the present day, the study of classical dynamical systems has concentrated on just such predictable cases. From the turn of this century, in the work of Poincaré, and with greatly accelerating progress in recent years, we have come to realize that 'tame' systems of this kind, open to prediction and control, are very untypical of dynamical behaviour. The typical case, on the contrary, involves such an infinitesimally balanced sensitivity to circumstance (one might almost say, such a degree of vulnerability) that it results in an almost infinitely multiplying variety of possible behaviours. How the system threads its way through this maze of possibilities is not open to prior prediction. As an example, consider the continued successive collisions of a collection of many billiard ball-like objects. One might suppose that to be a pretty well-determined system. However the way the balls emerge from each separate collision depends sensitively upon the precise details of the impact. Small uncertainties in the angle of incidence rapidly accumulate to produce exponentially diverging consequences. Molecules in a gas behave, in many ways, like small colliding billiard balls. After only 10^{-10} seconds, fifty or more collisions have taken place for each molecule. After even so few collisions the resulting outcome is so sensitive that it would be affected by the variation in the gravitational field due to an extra electron on the other side of the universe – the weakest force due to the smallest particle the furthest distance away! Predictability and control are very rapidly lost. We are necessarily ignorant of how such systems will behave. If you are a realist and believe, as I believe, that what we know (epistemology) and what is the case (ontology) are closely linked to each other, it is natural to go on to interpret this state of affairs as reflecting an intrinsic openness in the behaviour of these systems.[31] There is an emergent property of flexible process, even within the world of classical physics, which encourages us to see Newton's rigidly deterministic account as no more than an approximation to a more supple reality. The clockwork regularity of planetary motion, for so long taken to be the very paradigm of what goes on in the physical world, proves then to be just a singularly special sector within the general openness of physical process. Our primary human experience of sharing in that openness can only reinforce that view.

Such delicate systems are never truly isolated or self-contained. Causality cannot be strictly localized within them or within their constituent parts – once again the fragmentatory approach of reductionism is seen to be only part of the story. 'Downward causation', such as we experience when we will the movement of our arm, becomes a distinct possibility.[32] Arthur Peacocke is right to say that: 'There is no sense in which subatomic particles are to be graded as "more real" than, say, a bacterial cell or a human person, or even social facts.'[33] Every level of description is needed in our effort to do justice to the rich and varied process of the world, in its nature both flexible and reliable – including the category of divine providence. And every level of description may impose its own organizing pattern upon the flexibility of what can occur.

This is not the place to attempt to describe dynamical instabilities or the theory of chaos. It is sufficient to say that these modern dynamical insights do not result in just a descent into disorder but they also assert the possibility of the generation of a new order within their process (for example, by convergence upon what are called 'attractors').[34] We see emerging from this study of the dynamics of complex systems just those characteristics of structured openness which seem to offer hope that those super-complex systems, which are ourselves, might indeed manifest the freedom within regularity which is our basic human experience. And might not one go on to suppose that similarly the super-super-system of the cosmos might be capable, in an analogous way, of sustaining the operation of the acquiescent, economic and purposive wills of its Creator, within the flexibility of its lawful process?

Of course, a considerable extrapolation is needed beyond what we comprehend in order to reach an understanding of the capacity for human or divine action. I do not say that these age-old problems are solved, only that there is a hopeful direction in which to look for their solution. The rigid mechanism of nineteenth-century physics first began to dissolve with the discovery of the cloudy fitfulness of quantum theory. We now understand that even at those macroscopic levels where classical physics gives an adequate account, there is an openness to the future which relaxes the unrelenting grip of mechanical determinism. The universe may not look like an organism but it looks even less like a machine.

A consequence of the decay of predictability is a freedom for development, which enables physics to accommodate not only the idea of being (the timeless regularity of physical law) but also becoming (the evolving history of complex systems). The future is not already implied by the present. Time is no longer a mere index, parametrizing the inexorable disclosure of a determined state of affairs, but it more closely approximates to our psychological experience of its irreversible flow, with the fixity of the past but the openness of the future. Prigogine and Stengers say:

> Only when a system behaves in a sufficiently random way may the difference between past and future, and therefore irreversibility, enter into its description . . . The arrow of time is the manifestation of the fact that the future is not given, that, as the French poet Paul Valéry emphasized 'time is a construction'.[35]

The degree of randomness of which they speak arises from the labyrinthine possibilities open to an inherently undetermined complex system. They conclude their summary of the capacity for becoming, with which unstable dynamical systems far from equilibrium are endowed, by saying 'we can see ourselves as part of the universe we describe'.[36] This is no mere reductionist manner of speaking but the recognition that at last physics is beginning to be able to describe a world consonant with being the home of humankind. There is set before us the hope of a synthesis in which the perceived regularity of the physical world and the experienced freedom within ourselves are reconciled in an unfolding act of genuine becoming. Prigogine and Stengers chose for the title of their concluding chapter: 'From Earth to Heaven – the Reenchantment of Nature'.

The picture of God at work in the world within the flexibility of its process seems consonant with theological talk about his purposive immanent presence. John V. Taylor writes of the Creator-Spirit that:

> if we think of a Creator at all, we are to find him always on the inside of creation. And if God is really on the inside, we must find him in the process, not in the gaps. We know now that there are no gaps ... If the hand of God is to be recognized in His continuous creation, it must be found not in isolated intrusions, not in any gaps, but in the very process itself.[37]

I want to add to that the counterbalancing recognition of the transcendent Creator, who is the ground of those laws which make the cosmic process anthropically fruitful, whilst conceding that, without the corrective of the hidden working of the Spirit, that transcendent God would be left in deistic detachment. He is the God of both being and becoming.

The concept of divine immanent action helps us also to understand something of the scope of God's activity. Origen wrote that: 'It would be utterly absurd for a man who was troubled by the scorching sun at the summer solstice to imagine that by his prayer the sun could be shifted back to its springtime place among the heavenly bodies.' Maurice Wiles, from whom that quotation is culled, goes on to say 'Once that principle is acknowledged, it is difficult to define its limits',[38] and so he wants to discount the possibility of any specific action whatsoever. I agree that one cannot draw precise lines, but the notion of flexible process helps us to see where there might be room for divine manoeuvre, within the limits of divine faithfulness. The motions of the solar system are mechanical in nature, with a predictability over long periods of time which permits the construction of almanacs. Thus the succession of the seasons will be guaranteed by transcendent divine reliability and it would indeed be foolish to pray for their alteration. The generation of weather is a much more complex process, within which it is conceivable that small triggers could generate large effects. Thus prayer for rain does not seem totally ruled out of court. In this way one can gain some rough comprehension of the range of immanent action. It will always lie hidden in those complexes whose precarious balance makes them unsusceptible to prediction. The recently gained understanding of the distinction between physical systems which exhibit being and those which exhibit becoming[39] may be seen as a pale reflection of the theological dialectic of God's transcendence and God's immanence – consequences, respectively, of divine reliability and of the loving gift of freedom by the Creator.

We have been exploring how analogies with human action might be used to cast light on divine interaction with the world. We need also to recognize the differences which limit the applicability of such analogies. As physical systems we humans operate in ways which must be consistent with general physical principles, such as the conservation of energy and the thermodynamic relations (due to Brillouin and Szilard) which link information processing and storage to the necessary expenditure of a minimum quantity of energy (see p. 96). Since God is not embodied his knowledge is not subject to the latter restriction. (If it were, one would have to decide what is God's temperature. The natural cosmic answer would be the chilling one that it is the $3°K$ of the background radiation! One sees how odd divine embodiment becomes once one begins to look at it realistically.) Now consider the question of energy conservation. The labyrinthine bifurcating paths available to a complex dynamical system are not discriminated by energy differences. The simplest example of a bifurcation is the bead at the top of a vertical smooth U-shaped wire. It can fall either way, according to how it is slightly disturbed, with no energy barrier to induce preference for one side or the other. That is typical of much more complicated cases. If God acts in the world through influencing the evolution of complex systems, he does not need to do so by the creative input of energy. Of course, such divine energetic interaction is not to be excluded theologically, and it could be so hidden in complex process as not to be perceivable scientifically, but we have no need to invoke it. Moreover, it is probably wise not to do so, since it would risk turning God into a demiurge, acting as an agent among other agents.

Finally it is necessary to acknowledge that a subtle and respectful balance is required if the flexibility of physical process is to accommodate both God's action and our own and also the freedom of the universe to explore its own potential. How these intertwine and how each finds space for its own fulfilment without usurping the room necessary for the others, is a profound problem beyond our power to resolve in detail. It is a problem of which theology has long been aware, for it is the expression, in the widest cosmic terms, of the delicate dialectic of divine grace and creaturely freewill.

It is time to sum up. The clockwork universe is dead. The future is not just the tautologous spelling-out of what was already present in the past. Physics shows an openness to new possibility at all levels, from the microscopic (where quantum theory is important) to the macroscopic (where it is not). In that sense, physics describes a world of which we can conceive ourselves as being inhabitants. The division – quite as sharp as the Aristotelian division between celestial permanence and sub-lunar decay – which seemed to exist between the exterior world of inexorable process and the interior world of willed choice, is beginning to break down. We must not exaggerate the extent to which the two worlds are yet successfully integrated in our understanding. Many puzzles remain but there is a hopeful direction in which to look for their eventual reconciliation. The picture beginning to form encourages the thought of man as a psychosomatic unity, with the material and mental as complementary poles of his nature. In that way he is able to participate in a noetic world of ideas and purposes, as well as being able to act within the physical world. Such a view seeks to avoid an incomprehensible Cartesian dualism by its appeal to the complementary linkage of the material and mental as aspects of the world in different degrees of organizational complexity and flexibility. Here seems to be a promising location for the causal joints by which both we and God interact with the universe.

Speculative as all this is, remember that it appeals to the basic human experience of willed action, an ability which it interprets as arising from the open flexibility of the process of our bodies. Since there is also open flexibility within the general process of the world, it seems consistent to suppose that there is scope for action there also. In particular, it seems conceivable that this is the means by which God's purposive will may be exercised within his creation. Both we and God exercise the holistic power to influence, respectively, our bodies and the world by means of causal joints hidden within the unpredictability of process. Yet there are differences between human and divine participation in the world, that go beyond the contrast of scale between the limited and the Unlimited. The most important is that *we* are constituted by our physical bodies and so are in thrall to them. Their decay is our dissolution, though not without the Christian hope of a destiny beyond that dissolution through God's act of resurrection, reconstituting us in a new environment of his choosing. God, on the other hand, is not constituted by the cosmos, even in part of his nature, and so he is never in thrall to it. The expected eventual decay of this physical world will no more affect him than did its non-existence, if it was not there previous to the big bang. Though God interacts with the world it is not proper to speak of his being embodied in it.

It might be feared that this account is a return to the God of the gaps. In the pejorative sense of that term I do not think that this is the case. In the argument we have been at pains to exclude any appeal to God as just a physical agent among other agencies (p. 16). He is not an alternative source of energetic causation, competing with the effects of physical principles from time to time and overriding them. Rather we have tried to give those principles, as far as we know them, all due weight in the description of physical process, whilst recognizing that by themselves they do not constitute so tight a prescription of what happens that all scope for genuine becoming is removed from cosmic history. There is a sense in which all free action, ours or God's, depends upon 'gaps', the inherent incompletenesses which make openness possible, just as the resultant flexibilities require for their lasting significance that they be exercised within a generally reliable environment. God is the sustainer of the whole of his creation, the God of 'gaps' and regularities alike.

The purpose of this chapter has been to consider the extent to which modern science affords us scope to consider God's particular action, beyond his single Creatorly fiat. This consideration was necessary, not because science has an absolute right of veto over theology but because theology, truly conceived, seeks the most profound integration of all human knowledge, and so has to respect the offerings made to it by all branches of inquiry into the way things are. Our expectation that our action in the world might afford some analogical help in thinking about God's action has, with proper safeguards, proved valid. We have also seen that modern physics is not inimical to the undoubted possibility of our actions and so it does not exclude the possibility of God's actions either. It is possible with integrity, if not without puzzlement, to hold to what science has to say and still go on to consider those theological questions about God's action which must be our concerns in the chapters that follow.

3

Providence

Lesslie Newbigin has made an interesting suggestion about why it is that Eastern religions are enjoying popularity in our Western, scientifically influenced, culture. He says:

> The reason is clear. The Eastern religions do not understand the world in terms of purpose. The symbol of the dance is an interpretation of movement and change without invoking the idea of purpose. The Bible, on the other hand, is dominated by the idea of divine purpose.[1]

He fears that religion will settle for a *modus vivendi* with science, based on a division between a public world of fact and a private world of values. A false harmony would be achieved by relinquishing the idea of cosmic purpose, for 'if religion is construed in essentially mystical terms – that is, in terms for which the idea of purpose is not central – then there is no clash. The modern scientific world-view coexists peacfully and naturally with that sort of religion'.[2] The mystic's God, who is simply the sustaining ground of all being, is not so far from the deist's God, whose action is the single Creatorly fiat by which the world's process is sustained. They are, respectively, the immanent and transcendent poles of a detached deity, and neither is the personally purposive God of the Judaeo-Christian tradition. It is the claim of religious experience within that tradition to encounter such a personal God. Vernon White puts it in strong terms when he writes:

> We are not merely reacting to the conditions of the world; through them we are being acted upon. And this may be true of every event: as true of the experience of a routine day in Surbiton as of the day of a starving Sudanese peasant; as true of death as of life; as true of the smallest detail of any life as of the most momentous moments of history. Thus our deepest intuitions about the significance of every

moment of life are neither superstitious nor sentimental: they are rather the distilled glimpses of a divine activity which roams relentlessly and purposively through every constituent and category and contingency of this world.[3]

In the previous chapter we have contended that the scientific world-view, carefully considered, is not in fact hostile to the notion of a divine action bearing some analogous relation to the freedom enjoyed by human beings to execute their intentions. There is a flexibility within the open process of the universe which encourages us to think that this is a coherent possibility.

Of course, it is also true that, if there is a divine purpose at work in the world, part of its expression will certainly lie in the given created circumstance of that world. The scientific counterpart to the reiterated statement of the creation myth in Genesis, that God saw that it was good,[4] is the Anthropic Principle's recognition of the astonishing potentiality with which the laws of physics are endowed.[5] Let us recall just one example of the fruitful balance found in the universe's natural laws. If life were to be able to evolve there had to be some hydrogen left after those famous first three minutes in which the whole universe was an arena of nuclear reactions. Otherwise there could subsequently be no water, essential to life. When nuclear reactions started up again in the interior of stars, circumstances had to be such that some of those stars would explode, scattering into the environment heavier elements, such as carbon and iron, made in their cores and also needed for the evolution of life. These requirements together place a stringent limitation on the ratio of the weak nuclear force to the other forces of nature. That ratio cannot vary very much from the value we observe, if we are to be here to measure it. This is just one of the many anthropic balances necessary in the fundamental laws of physics if creation is to have the 'goodness' which is the capacity to evolve life. A rationally coherent explanation of why this should be so is beyond science's ability to offer, since it must take the laws of nature as its given starting-point. Such an explanation would be provided by theology's assertion that the finely balanced circumstance of the world stems from the benevolent purpose of its Creator.

If God is the origin of all that is, he is consistent with all that is, and this means that a great deal of his purposive activity will be hidden in the structure of scientific law. Hugh Montefiore, writing about the immanent activity of the Spirit in evolving creation, says:

> Although there is no external force imposed on species, and in particular on their genetic systems, mutations occur which would not be expected by random mutation. This is not because of external pressure, but because of the bias implanted in matter. Such bias is not, of course, to be detected by scientific measurement (and so the hypothesis is not testable) since there is no possibility of setting alongside it matter which is not implanted by the bias towards complexity and integration. Another way of describing this bias would be to call it the Holy Spirit working with the matter of the universe, unfolding the purposes of the Creator by immanent operation.[6]

Another way of describing the 'bias' would be (despite what Montefiore says in the third sentence of the quotation) simply to call it 'scientific law'. It is the way that matter actually *is*. There is no absolute expectation of randomness; the odds of chance events are to be calculated in relation to some lawful expectation. If I know the die is loaded I shall do my calculations differently from the way I would if I thought the die were true – and it is precisely a *scientific* question what sort of die it is that I am dealing with. If the Spirit is operating in the universe, part of his activity will certainly be through the scientific law which reflects his faithfulness and we do not have to picture him working against its grain. The God who is the ground of physical process is inescapably a *deus absconditus*, a hidden God. This is the area where Christian theism is 'necessarily tinged with deism'.

Yet cosmic history is not just a tautologous spelling-out of the consequences of the universe's laws and initial conditions. The world's freedom to become, and God's and our freedom to act within its unfolding process, derive from the flexibility resulting from the unpredictable sensitivity of response enjoyed by complex dynamical systems. A crude shorthand for the scientific account of one aspect of these matters is to refer to the interplay of chance and necessity. Necessity is the regular ground of possibility, expressed in scientific law. Chance, in this context, is the means for the exploration and realization of inherent possibility, through continually changing (and therefore at any time contingent) individual circumstances. It is important to realize that chance is being used in this 'tame' sense, meaning the shuffling operations by which what is potential is made actual. It is not a synonym for chaotic randomness, nor does it signify just a lucky fluke. Indeed, because he fears such overtones, Richard Dawkins ultimately rejects using the word in his account of evolutionary biology. He writes:

> The true explanation for the existence of life must embody the very antithesis of chance. The antithesis of chance is non-random survival [that is the sifting effect of necessity], properly understood. Non-random survival improperly understood, is not the antithesis of chance, it is chance itself . . . We have sought a way of taming chance, of drawing its fangs . . . To 'tame' chance means to break down the very improbable into less improbable components arranged in series.[7]

Dawkins is emphatic here, partly because he wishes to counter creationist claims that the evolution of life is so improbable that only divine *intervention* (that is, action against the natural grain) can explain it. He and I hold common cause in that, but I am still deeply impressed by the anthropic potentiality of the laws of nature which enable the small-step explorations of tamed chance to result in systems of such wonderful complexity as ourselves. It would not happen in 'any old world'. That the universe is capable of such fruitfulness speaks to me of a divine purpose expressed in the *given structure* of the world. That is an issue that the biologist Dawkins never addresses. On the other hand, the physicists Barrow and Tipler, in their magisterial survey of Anthropic Principle questions, devote considerable space to the discussion of teleology. They say:

> There is a general belief that teleology is scientifically bankrupt and that history shows it always to have been. We shall show that on the contrary, teleology has on occasion led to significant scientific advances. It has admittedly also led scientists astray; we want to study the past in order to learn under what conditions we might reasonably expect teleology to be a reasonable guide.[8]

Later they remark that 'the broad philosophical questions which teleology led people to ask early in this century . . . bear a striking resemblance to some of the questions now being attacked on the frontiers of modern cosmology and high energy particle physics'.[9]

The operation of chance, as I have described it, certainly need not imply that the ultimate outcome is totally unforeseeable or arbitrary. David Bartholomew has given a careful discussion of the necessary relationship between chance and certainty.[10] It is from this interrelationship that order rises out of chaos, as we see exemplified in the behaviour of dissipative systems which converge on to predictable limit cycles, approached along contingent paths.[11] Thus the sting is drawn from Jacques Monod's rhetorical assertion that 'pure chance, absolutely free but blind, is at the very root of the stupendous edifice of evolution'.[12] To acknowledge a role for tame chance is not in the least to deny the possibility that there is a divinely ordained general direction in which the process of the world is moving, however contingent detailed aspects of that progression (such as the number of human toes) might be.

Our concern so far in this chapter has been mainly with God's purpose and providence as seen in the general functioning of his creation. This results in a way of looking at the world which seeks to extract maximal meaning from universal process. If that kind of discourse speaks of acts of God it will be in relation to occasions when that underlying meaning is most transparently discerned. Maurice Wiles says of such events:

> In calling them special acts of God we would not be implying that there was any fundamental difference of the divine action to the particular worldly occurrences of their situation; we would be referring to the depth of response and the creative potential for eliciting further response from others embodied in those particular lives or those particular events.[13]

God's providence is then seen as a kind of teleological insight into general physical process. Providence is closely assimilated to creation. Indeed it becomes the everyday experience of the creative process in a world which is sustained in being by its Creator. Ian Barbour says of such ideas that 'it would be desirable to merge the traditional doctrines of creation and providence into a doctrine of *continuing creation*.[14]

It will be clear that I believe there to be important truth preserved in such a picture. It speaks of God's reliability and the way in which 'he makes his sun to rise on the evil and on the good, and sends rain on the just and the unjust'.[15] But it is not the whole truth, for it does not speak of that Fatherly care of God which must be concerned with the individual and his specific needs. Total impartiality would be total impersonality – which is not to say that a personal God has to have favourites, but that he will treat particular people in particular ways. Baelz reminds us that a notion of providence confined to overall generality is in danger of endorsing the idea of a God who 'sacrifices the individual on the altar of his cosmic plan'.[16] Though the evolutionary history of life has proved marvellously fertile, it shows scant concern for individual species, let alone particular creatures. Someone like Dawkins, who only reads that record, can conclude from it the chilling message that 'living organisms exist for the benefit of DNA rather than the other way round'.[17] So bleak a view will not do for Christian theology. Peter Baelz goes on to say that 'for the believer there can be no satisfaction with a general providence which is not also a special providence'.[18] Without the special providence, the idea of a personal God is emptied of content. Whatever it may mean to use personal language of God in an analogical sense, it surely cannot mean less than we experience of our own personhood, which is not content with general benevolence but seeks to meet individual need in individual ways. So White is right to protest that 'If God's purposive activity for the world is uniform and undifferentiated (except through particular creaturely response) then it is liable to be impersonal, amoral and relatively impotent'.[19]

Fortunately we do not have to accept the depersonalized God of deism. It is the burden of our tale that the scientifically discerned process of the world is sufficiently flexible to permit both God and us to work within it. When Bartholomew says that 'chance is seen as grist for the providential mill rather than as an obstacle to providential action'[20] he has in mind the opportunity afforded by the unpredictable openness of the physical universe.

Yet what a strange world it is that we enter when we listen to the stories the faithful tell about God's special care for them! A minister assures us that there is always a convenient empty parking meter available for him when he goes to the big city on the Lord's business. We might well think that the God who takes such trouble to save this man from minor inconvenience, might give a bit more attention to delivering his neighbour from the major disaster of liver cancer. If we truly detect God's providential acts they must surely be proportionate to the needs they meet. Otherwise we are caught in the trap that Ian Ramsey describes when he says: 'There is no limit to the absurdities that too narrow a view of providence can generate.'[21] At once we encounter the problem of theodicy and the mystery of differing individual destinies. Ramsey talks of two men in a covered wagon which is attacked by Indians. One man 'miraculously' survives the hail of arrows but his companion is killed. Ramsey comments: 'If the man in the covered wagon speaks genuinely of a special providence of God, his discourse about God must also incorporate the death of his friend.'[22] Quite so.

Much talk of special providence seems so selective and manipulative of what is happening. Austin Farrer illustrates this by an amusing tale 'of a simple old-fashioned piety, moving in a world of special providence confidently asserted and comically reassessed':

> Mr Jones' rheumatism was a judgement, until his daughter swore to you on the bible that the tale of his secret drinking was a baseless slander. Her father was a saint. His rheumatism was, therefore, a trial. But then the bowling club went on a day's outing and drove their charabanc into the sea; and Mr Jones' rheumatism, since it kept him home on the occasion, proved a blessing in disguise, and a providence indeed.[23]

At times, piety makes experience so plastic that it can be moulded into any edifying shape. One ends up, as Farrer says, with 'the God of kicks and halfpence'.[24]

Appeal to providence can also be used in the attempt to give divine endorsement to aspects of the world which might seem more likely to be permitted by his acquiescent will than to be brought about by his purposive will. Gregory of Nyssa thought that infant mortality was a providential weeding out of potential evil-doers. In our own day, we have heard confident assertions that AIDS is a direct judgement upon homosexual practices. All socially transmitted disease is a reminder that human acts have consequences which cannot be wished away, but a sign of divine displeasure which brought suffering also on the innocent (such as haemophiliacs) would seem a crude instrument for God to use.

Still, when all the caveats have been entered, Christian theology cannot do without a God who acts in the world by more than simply keeping it in being, for it looks to the One who brought Israel out of Egypt, raised Jesus from the dead, and to whom the early Church prayed 'while thou stretchest out thy hand to heal and signs and wonders are performed through the name of thy holy servant Jesus'.[25] These assertions are more than rhetorical flourishes embellishing descriptions of a time of political revolt, a recovery of nerve by demoralized disciples, and an exuberant start to a new movement. However obscure their modality, these events involve acts of God, or Christianity is profoundly in error.

Too glib an evocation of special providence may trivialize God's action in the world, but the rejection of all such particular action reduces God to the role of an impotent spectator. The religious mind strives to attain some balance, neither denying the perplexing variety of individual destiny nor failing to affirm that 'the Lord God omnipotent reigneth'.[26] The paradoxes of providence are not mere intellectual puzzles. They arise from the heart of religious experience. That experience has to wrestle with the fact of evil – Ricoeur went so far as to say that the book of Job speaks of 'the death of the God of Providence'[27] – yet that experience has also to wrestle with the fact of prayer, with its petition to God for action, and with the claim of miracle, that he has indeed acted in remarkable ways. These issues will have to be addressed in the chapters that follow.

Meanwhile we are able to endorse the intuitive feeling of Austin Farrer when he wrote: 'the grid of causal uniformity does not (to any evidence) fit so tight upon natural process as to bar the influence of an overriding divine persuasion'.[28] We are not condemned to a view of providence which simply sees it as 'best understood as a form of retrospective interpretation of experience',[29] a sort of pious hindsight which edifies but of which it can be said:

43

Understand that language of divine action too literally and the rich personal purpose which the language was designed to illuminate is undermined or diminished. For read such stories forwards instead of retrospectively and there is no escape from arbitrary election, implausible disposition of external circumstance and unacceptable manipulation of inner life.[30]

If there were no forward-moving story, the retrospectively claimed pattern would just be a trick of perspective. Providence would lie in the eye of the beholder and not in any act of God. If things just happen, then talk of divine initiative is in fact misleading. It is, of course, entirely likely that God's particular activity – hidden as it necessarily is within the unpredictable flexibility of cosmic process – is only discernible with hindsight, but that discernment must be the awareness of what has actually taken place as the result of the exercise of his will and it must not merely be our own imaginative construction. Because the causal joint of divine action is located in those regimes where what we call chance has a role to play, it may well involve events seeming to be characterizable as arbitrary or implausible. It may well be very diverse in its character, occurring where and when God can act without denying to his creation the freedom he has given to it to be itself. It is beyond our present knowledge to give a more detailed account of the possible range of divine action, but there is no reason to think that the physical world is so structured that God's particular activity is excluded from it.

The Christian understanding of providence steers a course between a facile optimism and a fatalistic pessimism. God does not fussily intervene to deliver us from all discomfort but neither is he the impotent beholder of cosmic history. Patiently, subtly, with infinite respect for the creation with which he has to deal, he is at work within the flexibility of its process.

44

4

Miracle

Much the bluntest claim that God acts in the world is made by those who assert that they believe in miracle. C. S. Lewis gives a 'crude and popular' definition of miracle as 'an interference with Nature by supernatural power'.[1] He goes on to acknowledge that this is not a theologian's definition. Let us also consider the definition offered by the philosopher of religion, Richard Swinburne, when he says that a miracle is 'an event of an extraordinary kind, brought about by a god, and of religious significance'.[12] An important qualification added by Swinburne is that of significance. A miracle is not just an astonishingly odd event, such as would be the sudden materialization in Trafalgar Square of a twelve-foot-high statue of Nelson made of chocolate. It has also to be the carrier of meaning. In the Johannine language of the New Testament, a miracle must be a 'sign'. The reason is clear. The only miracles that seriously could be said to be on the agenda are not just acts of a 'supernatural power' or 'a god'. They are the acts of God himself. He is no celestial conjurer, doing an occasional turn, but his actions must always be characterized by the deepest possible consistency and rationality. Therefore they must be endowed with meaning and be free from caprice. H. H. Farmer is right when he protests that: 'To define miracle . . . as an event involving suspension of natural laws is to begin in the wrong place. We must first ask what is the significance of miracle for religion.'[3] He goes on to quote a definition of miracle given by Huzinger: 'the phenomenal form of divine revelation'.[4] But surely that is drawn too widely. Two baskets of figs, one ripe, one unripe, were a vehicle of revelation to Jeremiah,[5] but we would hardly call them miraculous. Etymologically, a miracle is something wonderful. If it is to deserve the name it must be something totally contrary to common expectation, as is hinted at in Swinburne's circumspect phrase 'extraordinary' or by Lewis's stronger, un-compromising, words, 'an interference with Nature'.

It is with that word 'interference' that the troubles begin. We can imagine an agent of limited ability interfering with the work of another such agent. You construct a clock. I decide to modify its mechanism so that it no longer keeps me awake by striking the quarters at night. But if I am a perfectly skilful clockmaker I shall surely make for myself the perfect clock at my first attempt. God is not a demiurge, struggling to make the best of recalcitrant brute matter. He is the Creator and Sustainer of the whole physical world. Those very laws of nature, said to be violated by a miracle, are themselves the expression of his Creatorly will. One does not doubt, in one sense, his capacity to countermand them. Such action of itself cannot be beyond the power of an omnipotent God. Sir George Stokes robustly made the point in his Gifford Lectures of 1891, when he said: 'Admit the existence of a God, of a personal God, and the possibility of miracle follows at once. If the laws of nature are carried on in accordance with his will, he who willed them may will their suspension.'[6] Undoubtedly – but will the rationally coherent God actually change his mind? Will he really work against the grain of the natural law that he himself has ordained? And if *that* is what he does, why does he not do it more often? There seems to be plenty of scope for extra miracles to alleviate the sufferings of mankind. A theologically acceptable account of miracles will have to incorporate them within a total, and totally consistent, understanding of God's activity, and not see them as singular exceptions.

Thus I do not believe that interference is a fitting word to use about God's relation to his creation. The problem of miracle is twofold. One question is the nature of the evidence which might lead us to suppose that any particular event claimed as a miracle had actually happened. Another question is whether extraordinary events of the kind called miraculous can be any part of the faithful action of God. Is he not the God of reliable process and not of magic? Clearly the second question is prior to the first, since if miracle is an absurdity it is certainly not an act which God has actually performed. At the start of a discussion of whether Jesus was raised from the dead, I wrote:

> at best such an inquiry can point only to a balance of probability. In an event so contrary to normal expectation as the resurrection, the way in which the balance is weighed must depend on non-historical

factors . . . Ultimately one's attitude to the resurrection will depend upon the degree to which it does or does not cohere with one's general understanding of the way the world is.[7]

And that general coherence is necessary because we are considering the action of the one true God, who is the consistent ground of all that is. Having said that, I must go on to acknowledge that there is a certain amount of intellectual traffic in the opposite direction also. If there is evidence for miraculous events, that will stimulate our efforts to accommodate that possibility within a suitable metaphysical scheme. We are only too familiar from the scientific study of the physical world that our prior views of what is possible have frequently needed to be revised in the light of what is actually found to be the case. It is sufficient to utter the phrase 'quantum theory' to make the point. G. F. Woods wrote about miracle: 'I believe that to many minds the notion of uncaused events will be offensive.'[8] Yes indeed, but many physicists actually think of individual quantum events as being radically uncaused. I am not, of course, making the ridiculous argument that quantum theory is so counter-intuitive that after it anything goes. I am simply using it as a cautionary tale to warn us of our intellectual shortsightedness about the range of possibility.

The need to fit miracle within an extended pattern of God's reliable activity is no doubt a reason why there is a long history of thought that sees the miraculous as a kind of accelerated version of the natural. Augustine used this idea to talk about the water made into wine at Cana in Galilee.[9] What takes a season to accomplish in the vineyard is performed in a moment at the Lord's command. A miracle like the resurrection cannot be fitted into such a scheme, but it needs to be thought of instead as an anticipation of God's future destiny for all humanity. 'Christ has been raised from the dead, the first fruits of those who have fallen asleep'.[10] C. S. Lewis summarized this point of view when he wrote: 'Each miracle writes for us in small letters what God has already written, or will write, in letters too large to be noticed across the whole canvas of Nature.'[11] Seen as a striving after an harmonious reconciliation of the natural and the miraculous, the attempt attracts my sympathy, but I do not find it helpful in providing any detailed understanding of how that accord might be brought about. There is no real analogy between, on the one hand, the slow processes of organic chemistry by which water and elements from soil and air, together with energy from sunlight, combine to produce grape sugars, which then by the biochemical process of fermentation produce alcohol, and, on the other hand, the immediate transmutation of water into wine. If the latter actually occurred one does not suppose it to have happened by an incredibly speeded-up sequence of chemical reactions, produced by the catalytic presence of divine power. Our detailed understanding of the orderly processes of nature, and in particular of their intrinsic timescales, makes an accelerated naturalism more radically unnatural for us than it would have been for thinkers in the ancient world.

A similar instinct, to preserve a rational coherence within a miraculous setting, lies behind the attempt by the author of the Wisdom of Solomon to see the miracles of Israel's deliverance from Egypt as rearrangements of the natural order, so that 'as the notes of the lute can make various tunes with different names though each retains its own pitch, so the elements combined among themselves in different ways'.[12] Again one can applaud the motive without being helped by the actual insight proffered.

Once again, it is analogies with human action which seem most likely to be useful. Farmer speaks of miracle as 'God dealing with a unique and unrepeatable situation in an individual destiny; it is God knowing one in some sense by name', and he goes on to claim that miracle is 'the most intensely personal of all the categories of man's personal relationship with God'.[13] Certainly, within our own experience of persons, we know how it is possible for someone to act in a totally unexpected way, which nevertheless with hindsight we can see to have been consistent with his character.

God's action in this individual way might take two forms. The first is through 'arranged coincidence'. There are causal chains, lawfully propagating in the world, whose impingement upon each other can produce a situation of apparent significance. A man is in great distress of mind, plagued by feelings of guilt. He looks up into the sky and the continually changing pattern of the clouds at that moment assumes a form which, from his perspective, looks like the representation of a cross upon a hill. That man may feel that God has indeed spoken to him by name, recalling to his thought the redeeming death of Christ. He does not need to assume that cloud pattern to have been hastily assembled by divinely dispatched cherubim. He thankfully accepts the experience of a highly significant coincidence.

That imaginary example has a slightly bizarre air about it, but many people would claim to have experienced events which are not contrary to natural process but which, in their detailed character, have nevertheless seemed to be carriers of divinely conveyed meaning. It is persuasive to consider in this way the nature miracles of the Gospels, such as the stilling of the storm.[14] Jung made a study of events of this kind occurring in the lives of his patients, which he attributed to the 'acausal connecting principle' of synchronicity. He wrote that:

> The problem of synchronicity has puzzled me for a long time, ever since the middle twenties, when I was investigating the phenomena of the collective unconscious and kept coming across connections which I simply could not explain as chance groupings or 'runs'. What I found were 'coincidences' which were connected so meaningfully that their 'chance' concurrence would represent a degree of improbability that would have to be expressed by an astronomical figure.[15]

He goes on to give an example of a patient who was telling him of an important dream in which she had been given a golden scarab. At that very moment Jung heard a tapping on the window and, opening it, found outside a scarabeid beetle which, contrary to its normal habits, was trying to enter the darkened room.

It is, of course, very difficult to know how, in all sobriety, to estimate the odds against such significant occurrences. So many things might happen which might be taken as having meaning, and since things are happening all the time, are there not in the end bound to be some events looking like synchronicity? There is the danger of the same sort of plasticity of interpretation which we noted in relation to simple appeals to providence (p. 42). The problem of odds is more difficult than Jung seems to allow. Nevertheless, I do not think one can deny that there are remarkable threads of coincidence to be found in human life which it is proper for those who experience them to interpret as the personal God calling them by name. We may suppose these happenings to be brought about by that sensitive openness of the world's process, which in Chapter 2 we suggested might be the vehicle of both God's providential care and of our own interaction with the world. Because of their unique significance to those who have experienced them, we can understand why those involved may want to speak of those occurrences as 'miraculous', but it is clear that properly speaking they are to be thought of as acts of providence.

The second way in which we might conceive that God interacts with individuals is more closely connected with the concept of miracle, as it was expressed in the definitions at the beginning of this chapter. Here something happens which is not the unexpected concurrence of two perfectly expectable lines of development, but rather an event takes place of a radically unexpected character, through and through. What happens is not something that can be thought of as arising from the inherent flexibility of process, but it is something totally contrary to the previously known character of that process. The resurrection would be an outstanding example of such a miracle, truly so-called. Not only do dead men stay dead in our common experience, but it is inconceivable that the exploitation of 'chance' enabled a dead man to live again, nevermore to die.

I am carefully trying to characterize the event as 'unexpected' rather than using discontinuous language like 'due to direct divine intervention'. In other words, I can go as far as Swinburne's 'extraordinary' but not to the length of Lewis's 'an interference with nature'. My reason is simply that I believe that God's complete action in the world must be consistent throughout. In the end there is no sharp separation to be made between general providence and special providence and miracle. God's relation to this world is not like ours to our bodies, where there are autonomic processes, such as the circulation of the blood, which go on without the explicit exercise of our will (and which in God's case, if the analogy were valid, would be called laws of nature or general providence), together with other, explicitly willed, acts (which in God's case would be called special providence or miracle). The discontinuities which the language of natural and miraculous suggest, or the divisions between God's types of will, are matters of human convenience, relating to the differences in our perception and not to fundamentally distinct kinds of activity in God.

We are familiar in many branches of knowledge with the utility of dividing up what we know at root to be a fundamental unity. Levels of behaviour which are always present may only be visible in particular regimes. The laws of nuclear force act all the time and are indispensable in maintaining the stability of matter, yet we are only aware of their operation when we enter a regime of sufficiently high energy where, for instance, nuclear transmutations become possible which are not observable in ordinary circumstances. Nowhere in the world was there a nucleus with atomic number greater than 92 until the specially contrived circumstances brought about at the Radiation Laboratory at Berkeley permitted the formation of a series of transuranic elements. Sometimes such changes of circumstance can produce radically different modes of behaviour. One example, too familiar to surprise us but remarkable nevertheless, is the way in which the slow increase of temperature suddenly produces a discontinuous change from liquid to gas at boiling point. The detailed physics of such phase changes (as they are called) are notoriously difficult to figure out, but certainly the underlying laws of nature do not change at 100° centigrade.

That example of the discontinuous change of behaviour with changing physical regime, coupled with the unbroken regularity of physical law, may be of some small analogical help in thinking how God might be capable of acting in miraculous, radically unexpected, ways, whilst remaining the Christian God of steadfast faithfulness. That is the fundamental theological problem of miracle: how these strange events can be set within a consistent overall pattern of God's reliable activity; how we can accept them without subscribing to a capricious interventionist God, who is a concept of paganism rather than of Christianity. Miracles must be perceptions of a deeper rationality than that which we encounter in the every day, occasions which make visible a more profound level of divine activity. They are transparent moments in which the Kingdom is found to be manifestly present.[16]

For all its stark contradiction of normal expectation, the resurrection is readily accommodated in Christian theology within such a consistent account of God's action in Christ. It was fitting that he whom uniquely 'God made both Lord and Christ' should be raised up because 'it was not possible that he should be held by the pangs of death'.[17] Much more difficult is a claimed occurrence like the turning of water into wine at Cana in Galilee. At one level it seems an over-reaction to a mild social problem arising from inadequate prior provision. At a somewhat deeper level, it is an acted parable of the transforming power of Christ, but performed in a self-conscious way which does not square easily with the hidden and unforced nature of Jesus' ministry. Christians will take different views on this particular question, but it is clear where the debate lies. Mere wonderworking, without an underlying consistency of action and intent, would never be a credible Christian miracle.

The concept of regime, of the sensitive relationship of possibility to circumstances, can also help us to understand something of why miracles occur so sparsely and with a seeming fitfulness. If God is consistent he must act in the same way in the same circumstances, but personal matters are so infinitely graded in their characters that what may seem closely similar occasions can in fact be quite different from each other. In one place Swinburne defines a miracle as 'a non-repeatable exception to the operation of nature's laws, brought about by God'.[18] Clearly the discontinuous language of 'exception' is exactly what we are trying to avoid, and the word 'unrepeatable' has about it that air of arbitrariness which we are at pains to reject. It can be saved from that if we interpret it as referring to that subtle complexity of human circumstance which implies that personal events are never repetitions of their predecessors. Every human experience is unique. Presumably Farmer had something like this in mind when he wrote: 'It is part of the essential personal quality of the awareness of miracle that it should be in any one experience comparatively rare.'[19] Seldom will the circumstances be just right for the emergence of the unexpected. (That remark is saved from mere tautology by its pointing to the ground that permits miracle to happen.) There remains, of course, the very difficult question of why miracle should be so *exceedingly* rare, when we consider the multitude of agonizing occasions which might be thought to call for its assistance. People say that they cannot at all believe in a God who acts if he did not do so to stop the Holocaust. If God were a God who simply interferes at will with his creation, the charge against him would be unanswerable. But if his action is self-limited by a consistent respect for the freedom of his creation (so that he works only within the actual openness of its process) and also by his own utter reliability (so that he excludes the shortcuts of magic) it is not clear that he is to be blamed for not overruling the wickedness of humankind.

Some further answer might lie in the very specific qualities required of a regime if it is to be able to exhibit what we call the miraculous. The Gospels portray one aspect of this when they record that at Nazareth Jesus 'could do no mighty work there . . . and he marvelled at their unbelief'.[20] His healings were not just naked acts of power imposed without the collaborative assent of those to be healed. Augustine discussed: 'Why, it is asked, do miracles never occur nowadays, such as occurred (you mention) in former times?'[21] He thought, in fact, that some had occurred in his own time (he gives examples) but that they were more frequent in apostolic times because they were then necessary to launch the Christian gospel, which subsequently could propagate without such aid. C. S. Lewis makes a similar point about the necessary aptness of historical circumstance when he writes chillingly that:

> God does not shake miracles at Nature at random as if from a pepper-castor. They come on great occasions: they are found at the great ganglia of history – not of political or social history, but of that spiritual history which cannot be fully known by men . . . Miracles and martyrdoms tend to bunch together about the same areas of history.[22]

There are those who would interpret this phenomenon in a different way. They would say that miracles 'occurred' at times of particular ignorance and credulity, or occasions when heady excitement suspended sober judgement. Miracles always seem to happen at some other place, and some other time, than here and now. That challenge reminds us of the first of the two general questions we raised earlier. Our discussion so far has sought to show that miracles are neither ruled out by scientific knowledge that the world is a relentlessly inflexible mechanism (it is not) nor by theological knowledge that God is just the deistic upholder of general process (he is more than that). That there may have been miracles is a coherent possibility. Whether there actually have been is a question we have still to address.

It is not my present purpose to engage in a study of individual claims for miraculous happenings. I have elsewhere attempted to show why I believe in the central Christian miracle of the resurrection of Christ.[23] Now I want to discuss the general considerations which are involved in weighing the evidence. A convenient method is to engage in dialogue with that resolute sceptic, David Hume. He says: 'a miracle is a violation of the laws of nature; and as firm and unalterable experience has established these laws, the proof against miracle, from the very nature of the fact, is as entire as any argument from experience can possibly be imagined.'[24] It is rather touching to find the stern critic of induction placing such firm faith in the unalterable character of nature's laws. The idea that they are totally known, and totally inflexible in their consequence, has been sufficiently rebutted in what has gone before for us to be able to pass on immediately to the four arguments which Hume alleges against there ever having been a miracle. They are:

1 The lack of adequate historical testimony by 'a sufficient number of men, of such unquestioned good sense, education, and learning, as to secure us against all delusion'. The extraordinary standard of evidence that Hume demands is exemplified by a case which he discusses later:

> There surely never was a greater number of miracles ascribed to a person, than those which were lately said to have been wrought in France upon the tomb of Abbé Paris . . . The curing of the sick, giving hearing to the deaf, and sight to the blind, were everywhere talked of as the usual effects of that holy sepulchre. But what is more extraordinary; many of the miracles were immediately proved upon the spot, before judges of unquestioned integrity, attested by witnesses of credit and distinction, in a learned age, and on the most eminent theatre that is now in the world. Nor is this all: a relation of them was published and dispersed everywhere; nor were the *Jesuits*, though a learned body, supported by the civil magistrate, and determined enemies to those opinions in whose favour the miracles were said to be wrought, ever able directly to refute or detect them.

What is Hume's conclusion from this remarkable testimony, which might have been thought to originate from 'a sufficient number of men, of such unquestioned good sense, education and learning'? It is complete denial of its authenticity, based solely on 'the absolute impossibility of a miraculous nature of the events'. Hume turns out to be an absolutist in the matter, an intransigent sceptic who would *never* accept any evidence contradicting his prior expectation. There is no arguing with such an entrenched position, but its adoption is the antithesis of being open to the truth. It is certainly uncongenial to the habits of thought of a scientist.

Circumstantial accounts of apparently miraculous events continue to be reported. A recent case involved a lady who was paralysed from her left hip to her toe, owing to an injury. Eventually the doctors concluded that they could do no more for her and she must reconcile herself to being an invalid for the rest of her life, able to walk only with the greatest difficulty. In 1980 a healing mission was held in a local church. The lady was induced to meet the priest conducting it, though she is said to have been 'bitter, disillusioned and completely lacking in faith'. At their second encounter she had a strange visionary experience in which an elderly monk took her by the hand and commanded her repeatedly 'In the name of Jesus, walk'. From that moment she was able to walk, jump and bend down, completely without pain. Her husband, an orthopaedic charge nurse, on examining his wife, found that a large ulcer, which he had been dressing, had also healed spontaneously.[25] Whatever one makes of this remarkable story, it cannot simply be dismissed on a priori grounds as not having possibly happened.

2 The human desire for the astonishing is such that 'The passion of *surprise* and *wonder*, arising from miracles, being an agreeable emotion, gives a sensible tendency towards belief in these events, from which it is desired.' Certainly there is cause for caution here, which needs to be taken seriously. I am not disposed to take at face value those remarkable, and apparently circumstantial, stories which circulate in our day, about extraterrestrial visitors who arrive in flying saucers. It is noteworthy, though, that the miracles in the Gospels, while frequently being said to arouse amazement among the bystanders, are recounted in a way that is spare and matter of fact. The comparison with the fanciful tales in the apocryphal Gospels is very striking in this respect. Hume thinks that 'if the spirit of religion join itself to the love of

wonder, there is an end of common sense'. If there are unusual regimes with unusual phenomena, then there will indeed have to be an end to common sense, in order to do justice to the novel nature of that particular aspect of reality. I have already suggested that science delivers us from an undue tyranny of everyday expectation. Common sense is not a Procrustean bed into which all experience must be made to fit. Even that human desire for wonder, against which Hume warns us, may be an instinctive longing for something beyond what meets the routine eye, a religious intuition which may find its true confirmation in the encounter with God. I think that part of the popularity of modern science fiction, with its talk of other worlds and other beings, lies in its ministering to a suppressed longing to meet the One who is other than us.

3 'It forms a strong presupposition against all supernatural and miraculous relations, that they are observed chiefly to abound among ignorant and barbarous nations.' We may not feel today quite the same degree of confidence, presumed by the men of the Enlightenment, in drawing the line between civilization and barbarism. It might be that other cultures provide, through their different practice and different kinds of openness, regimes more conducive than ours to certain types of experience. I understand that some of the most remarkable instances claimed to demonstrate telepathy have occurred among the Lapps. If there is indeed such a faculty for human communication, it is not inconceivable that it might have been best preserved among those who live a simple life in sparsely populated regions, and to have atrophied among those who live in close contact with their neighbours and with a telephone to hand.

I am not denying that the ancient world may have been more uncritically receptive of strange stories than we are today, and that caution must be exercised because of that. After surveying accounts of insurgents such as Theudas, wonderworkers such as Apollonius of Tyana, Jewish charismatics like Honi the circle-drawer, and the writings of the magical papyri, E. P. Sanders says:

> Miracles were sufficiently common, sufficiently diverse, and
> sufficiently scattered among holy men, messianic pretenders,
> magicians and temples that we cannot draw any inference from

them in order to explain what social type Jesus fits best or what his intention really was.[26]

The picture is of an ancient world where claims of the unusual were rather widespread. Yet there is also in Scripture a tradition of incredulity. Abraham cannot wait for the son of the promise and so he has a child by Hagar, his wife's maid.[27] Zechariah is incredulous when a similar promise of a son is made to him.[28] Thomas will not accept the testimony of his friends that they have met the risen Lord.[29] The Gospel of Matthew, often so triumphalist in tone, ends with an appearance of the risen Jesus in Galilee where we are told that 'when they saw him they worshipped him but some doubted (*edistasan*)'.[30] Jesus rejects the idea of miracle as coercive of belief,[31] refuses a request for a sign,[32] and seldom appeals to his acts.[33] The Gospel stories are remarkably free from the sort of embellishment that appeals to the credulous. They are also remarkably free from appeal to miracle as knockdown argument. Even the empty tomb needs interpretation.[34]

The theological need to understand miracle within a consistent pattern of God's action means that there is little appeal to it today as a *primary* ground for belief (except for the critical role that the resurrection plays in Christian thought, as the vindication of the crucified Messiah and of the God who allowed his chosen one to die a shameful death). Exceptions have first to be tested against a previously established rule, God's miraculous acts evaluated in relation to the experience of his continuing faithfulness. Richard Swinburne is one of the few modern writers to defend a major role for miracle as the foundation of belief. He summarizes his conclusion by saying: 'Paley writes "In what way can a revelation be made, but by miracles? In no other way which we are able to conceive." I have argued that Paley is right.'[35] It seems to me, however, that it is only as we come to know God in his creation and providence, in prayer and worship, in Christ and in the Church, that we shall be able to accommodate within the grand sweep of that revelation those particular actions that are called miracles.

4 Hume felt that the claims of all the competing world religions to have experienced the miraculous, thereby cancelled each other out:

> Every miracle, therefore, pretended to have been wrought in any of these religions (and all of them abound in miracles), as its direct

scope is to establish the particular system to which it is attributed; so it has the same force, though more indirectly, to overthrow every other system. In destroying a rival system, it likewise destroys the credit of those miracles in which the system was established; so that all the prodigies of different religions are to be regarded as contrary facts, and the evidence of these prodigies, whether weak or strong, as opposite to each other.

The argument supposes the total opposition of one religion to another; the impossibility, say, that the Christian God should honour the prayer of a Hindu worshipper. Whatever the true relation of the world's religions may be to each other – and that is one of the most perplexing and urgent problems that theology faces today – it cannot be that God has left himself without power and presence in relation to the majority of humanity for most of the time. The Christian is not led to deny that God acts in personal encounter with those of other faiths.

Archdeacon Paley made a judicious comment on Hume's whole attitude when he wrote:

> Mr Hume states the case to be a contest of opposing improbabilities; that is to say, a question whether it be more improbable that the miracle should be true or the testimony false: and this I think is a fair account of the controversy. But herein I remark a want of argumentative justice, that in describing the improbability of miracles he suppresses those circumstances of extenuation, which result from our knowledge of the existence, power and disposition of the Deity.[36]

And that is it. 'The fundamental problem' as Mary Hesse says, 'is not about miracle but about transcendence',[37] about whether God is in any detailed and active way the ruler of his creation. If he is, then his activity, though always utterly consistent, may sometimes be totally unexpected. As Charlie Moule says, 'the focus of the whole discussion' is 'where and within what bounds do we look for consistency?'[38] We have sought to show that modern science does not draw those bounds so tightly that there is no scope for the particular action of a personal God.

5

Evil

The more strongly one is able to speak of God's particular action in the world, the more firmly one asserts that world to be subject to his purposive will, so much the more forceful becomes the problem of the widespread existence of evil within it. The dilemma was noted in ancient times. Lactantius quotes Epicurus as putting the point with admirable clarity, three centuries before Christ: 'God either wishes to take away evils, and is unable; or He is able, and is unwilling; or He is neither able nor willing; or He is both willing and able.' That is, God is either less than wholly powerful, or less than wholly good, or less than both, or, if he is both wholly powerful and good 'from what source then are evils? or why does He not remove them?'[1] While the problem has been debated for more than two millennia, it is one that is felt with particular intensity today. I suppose the problem of evil and suffering to be the one that more than any other holds many people back from belief in God. Those of us who are believers are perpetually aware of the challenge that it presents to our faith.

In the Old Testament, the prosperity of the wicked is quite as much a difficulty as the unmerited suffering of the righteous. 'I was envious of the arrogant, when I saw the prosperity of the wicked' says the psalmist, so that he was tempted to think that 'All in vain have I kept my heart clean and washed my hands in innocence'. The only resolution to be found lay in the recognition of the transience of the wicked's triumph: 'Truly thou dost set them in slippery places: thou dost make them fall in ruin.'[2]

The classic scriptural exploration of the plight of the just man unjustly afflicted is to be found in the Book of Job, but the answer that Job receives in the end is neither explanation nor justification but the voice from the whirlwind that humbles him before his Creator and the mystery of creation. In the New Testament suffering is seen as 'the fiery ordeal which comes upon you to prove you', and as a participation in those messianic woes that herald the end of history, so that the Christian is bidden to 'rejoice in so far as you share Christ's sufferings, that you may also rejoice and be glad when his glory is revealed'.[3]

Both Old and New Testaments set before us the hope of a world eventually redeemed from suffering, in which 'they shall not hurt nor destroy in all my holy mountain'[4] and 'death shall be no more, neither shall there be mourning nor crying nor pain any more'.[5] But they both accept the existence of suffering in this present world as a given fact. The psalmists protest to God with great boldness – 'Rouse thyself! Why sleepest thou, O Lord?'[6] – but they do not utter that modern cry 'It isn't fair'. The biblical acceptance of the strange mixture of good and evil present in the world is articulated with startling directness by Second Isaiah, when God says:

> I form light and create darkness,
> I make weal and create woe,
> I am the Lord, who do all these things.[7]

According to Peter Baelz, J. S. Mill closed the Bible in dismay when he came to these words.[8]

They were received with greater enthusiasm by C. G. Jung. He perceived in the human psyche that dark side which he called 'the shadow'. By analogy, he believed there was a corresponding antinomy within the divine nature, which he thought was unveiled in the Book of Job. When the Lord proposes the conundrum 'Who is this that darkens counsel by words without knowledge?'[9] in Jung's view 'it is Yahweh himself who darkens his own counsel and who has no insight'.[10] 'With brazen countenance he can project his shadow side and remain unconscious at man's expense.'[11] For Jung the problem of evil is solved by incorporating it within the divine nature. But that will not do. No doubt it is the case that our own rejected shadow contains elements whose reconciliation is a necessary part of our attaining wholeness, but to speak of God in similar terms is surely an undue surrender to anthropomorphism. The God of Jung, exploring his psyche in encounter with Job, is really a Homeric god in modern dress, with all the limitation and ambiguity that implies. There has always been a specious attraction in dualism as the answer to the perplexing mixture of good and evil that we find in the world around us. Jung's divine antinomies are a sophisticated form of dualism, incorporated within the one divine nature. Such a God is not the one that Jesus taught us to address with confidence as 'Abba, Father'. Before we accept the ambiguous God of Jungian thought, we must explore alternative approaches to understanding the problem of evil.

An early Christian thinker to wrestle with the problem was Augustine. In Book 7 of the *Confessions* he fully acknowledges the difficulty of the apparent conflict concerning divine power and divine goodness. 'Where then does evil come from, if God made all things, and, because he is good, made them good too?' He rejects the idea that there is no real evil, for 'If so, why do we fear and guard against something which is not there? . . . either there is evil and we fear it, or the fear itself is evil.'[12] For Augustine the answer lay, not in a Jungian redefinition of the nature of God, but in a redefinition of the nature of evil. It is not an illusion, but it is not true reality either, for evil is *privatio boni*, the absence of the good, an idea that Augustine got from Plotinus. Thus evil is non-being, just as darkness is not a positive entity but the absence of light. (There are photons, particles of light, but there are not scotons, particles of darkness.) 'For evil is not a positive substance: the loss of good has been given the name of evil.'[13]

For all its intellectual attractiveness, this is a very difficult theory to square with experience. How could one tell a victim of cancer or the Holocaust that he was simply suffering from the privation of the good? There seems to be a much more positive quality to evil than Augustine's theory allows. Yet there is also a deep human intuition that, though evil is real, it is not the ultimate reality. Peter Berger draws our attention to the familiar scene of a mother comforting her child who has woken frightened in the night. Essentially her message is: 'Don't be afraid – everything is in order, everything is all right.' Berger analyses this formula and concludes that it can

without in any way violating it, be translated into a statement of cosmic scope – 'Have trust in being'. This is precisely what the formula intrinsically implies. And if we believe the child psychologists (which we have good reason to do in this case), this is an experience that is absolutely essential to the process of becoming a human person. Put differently, at the very centre of the process of becoming fully human, at the centre of *humanitas*, we find an experience of trust in the order of reality. Is this experience an illusion? Is the individual who represents it a liar?[14]

I, for one, must answer 'no' to these questions. If we are to have trust in being, that trust must ultimately be grounded in the One who is Being himself, for anything less is subject to change and decay. The ambiguous God of Jung would not be adequate ground for such reliance. Something like the *chesed*, the steadfast love of the God of the Jews and Christians, is needed. Thus we find ourselves living out the existential counterpart of the intellectual dilemma with which this chapter opened. The terrible character of evil is not to be denied, but it is to be endured relying on him who is the hope of them that are past hope. Peter Baelz is close to the heart of the matter when he says that there is a 'subtle dialectic of rebellion and acceptance in the Christian response to suffering and evil'.[15]

The Augustinian proposal that evil is the privation of the good acknowledges this asymmetry between good and evil, trust and despair, which characterizes human experience. Yet it fails fully to grapple with the agonizing intensity of the problem presented by the degree of suffering encountered in a world which is held to be the creation of a good and powerful God. The more fully God is identified with the world, the more fully this problem presents itself. It seems to me that evil is a great difficulty for any theory of the total or partial embodiment of God in the universe. Grace Jantzen denies this. She believes that it is 'not a greater or even a different problem for this view than for a cosmic dualist'. This is because 'Unless one is willing to adopt a Manichaean view, in which the material universe is irreducibly other than God, one must affirm in some sense "God is All", all things have their origin in God, and hence evil itself is in God.' This does not turn God into the devil because:

> we can make a distinction between saying that evil is in God and that God himself is evil. God is evil if, to use a Kantian term, he has an evil will: that is, if there is nothing to justify the evil for which he is ultimately responsible and which could not exist but for him.[16]

I want to suggest that Jantzen states the alternatives too starkly. There is a relationship of God to the world which is neither embodied nor Manichaean, but which is Creatorly, and which is in its nature superior to both in affording some understanding of how it may be possible 'to justify the evil for which he is ultimately responsible'. There are insights of theodicy which depend upon God's gift of freedom to be itself, given to the whole world not just to humankind, which do not seem to be available to panentheistic argument. The creation is seen to be other than God, but not radically opposed to him in a Manichaean way.

There is only one broad strategy possible for any theodicy. It is to suggest that the world's suffering is not gratuitous but a necessary contribution to some greater good which could only be realized in this mysterious way. The problem of evil is to be met by setting it within that wider context in which it can dissolve into fulfilment. This is the tradition of *felix culpa*, by which great disaster is perceived as disaster but yet also as the ground of a greater good. John Hick says that what Christian thought must always reject is 'the idea of finally *wasted* suffering and goodness' and he calls *felix culpa* 'one of the cornerstones of Christian theodicy'.[17]

There are those who deny that this approach is possible; in their view the debt of suffering can never be paid off by any future credit. Dorothy Soelle bluntly says: 'No heaven can rectify Auschwitz.'[18] The classic statement of this case against theodicy is made by Ivan Karamazov in Dostoevsky's novel. After recounting the terrible tale of a Russian general who allowed an eight-year-old peasant boy to be torn to pieces by his hounds as a revenge for the child's having slightly injured one of them, Ivan says:

Listen: if all have to suffer to buy eternal harmony by their suffering, what have children to do with it - tell me please? It is entirely incomprehensible why they should have to buy harmony by their sufferings.

and he goes on to say:

too high a price has been placed on harmony. We cannot afford to pay so much for admission. And therefore I hasten to return my ticket of admission.[19]

Certainly this dreadful story is not to be explained away by any glib invocation of future bliss. Yet if Augustine was mistaken in believing that 'God judged it better to bring good out of evil, than to suffer no evil to exist',[20] then this world is indeed one without meaning and hope. The mystery of suffering is great, but so is the mystery of persisting hope. In the Book of Revelation it is the *martyrs* who cry 'Salvation belongs to our God who sits on the throne, and to the Lamb'.[21] So Richard Creel is right to say that: 'The seeming meaninglessness, absurdity and waste of innocent suffering and tragic loss are overcome only in the existence of God. To be sure the Holocaust was enormously tragic – but without God it is even more tragic.'[22]. He goes on to say that 'This seems to me to be a terribly important point that Dostoyevsky's Ivan failed to consider' and he criticizes Ivan for seeming 'more concerned that his cynicism be vindicated than that the innocent be redeemed.'[23]

The most blithe approach to the problem of suffering finds its expression in Leibniz's confidence that this is, in fact, the best of all possible worlds. It is very doubtful that that idea is any more coherent than the idea of the greatest possible work of art. It is pointless to argue whether the *Missa Solemnis* is superior to the *Mass in B Minor*, or vice versa, but it is clear that both are musically to be preferred to lesser works. If the universe is to be the worthy creation of the one true God, then it must have about its process the authenticity that we find in great art. Its discords must be part of a greater harmony.

Part of the essential character of a work of art is its triumph over the limitations imposed by its medium – the painting's representation of a three-dimensional world on two-dimensional canvas; the sculptor's representation of life and movement in static stone; the play or novel's exploration of a human life in half a dozen episodes; music's wonderful capacity to speak of eternity by a temporal sequence of sounds. 'The best of all possible worlds' need not be a world altogether free from hardship to be endured or difficulties to be overcome. The problem of evil and suffering is a problem of scale, not of simple existence. The pain which guards the child from damage in the fire is also the excruciating pain which manifests itself too late for the cancer victim to be cured of it. The sorrows and deprivations of life, which in due measure might spur us to beneficial effort, are often experienced as burdens so heavy that they can only subdue and diminish. It is in these matters of degree that the issue of evil is confronted.

There are two forms of evil that are present in the world – moral and natural.[24] Moral evil arises from the willed choices of humankind. It encompasses man's inhumanity to man, from the domestic cruelties of parent upon child, to the national cruelties of oppression and racial discrimination, to the global cruelties of exploitation and starvation. Dreadful as the resulting sufferings are, their immediate source is clear. They result from the exercise of human will. Men and women are directly responsible for them. That responsibility may be diffused, for we are all subject to the pressures of society and of our upbringings, but it is primarily located in humanity. The classic answer to the allowed existence of moral evil is the free-will defence – the claim that it is better for God to have created a world of freely choosing beings, with the possibility of their voluntary response to him and to each other, as well as the possibility of sinful selfishness, than to have created a world of blindly obedient automata. This is held to be so despite the great suffering brought about by the abuse of that free will. How one can weigh the matter is beyond nice calculation, but it is a fundamental human intuition that we are better as we are, in all our flawedness, than we would be if we were reduced to automatic action, however beneficially programmed that action might be. The widespread, and right, reluctance to countenance coercive measures like the castration of persistent sex-offenders, is testimony to this intuitive respect for the value of human freedom, however it may be perverted to destructive ends.

Some have criticized the free-will defence by alleging that it should not be beyond the ingenuity of an omnipotent God to create beings who are free but *always* freely choose the right. Indeed, if that is not the case, does it not mean that the Christian hope of an eventual triumph of the Kingdom of God is incoherent? Unless that Kingdom is populated by just such beings, will it not be perpetually precarious and never secure? If God is a God who, out of respect for his creation, acts through process and not by magic, then we must distinguish between what is initially possible and what is eventually possible. In terms of naked power, no doubt God could have created humankind fully fleshed, rather than allowing them to emerge after fifteen billion years of cosmic history, but he did not do so. That is the patient way that Love works. Equally it may only be in accord with God's nature to produce redeemed humanity through its experience of this 'vale of soul making', rather than at a divine stroke. (Hence the importance of a demythologized doctrine of purgatory.) John Hick has given a careful discussion of these issues.[25] He poses the question 'Is it logically possible for God so to make men that they will freely respond to Himself in love and trust and faith?', to which he gives the answer 'no'.[26] His argument is based on the contrast between hypnotically induced acts of apparent friendliness and true friendship. The former is analogous to what God would have brought about in the act of creation being suggested; the latter is what he is actually seeking through humanity's truly free response to him. Surely it is this second possibility which is the greater good.

There remains the problem of natural evil. Tempest and earthquake take their toll of human life. Though the incidence of some disease may be due to human action – for example, through the carcinogenic effects of pollution – yet the far greater part is surely the responsibility of the Creator alone. He is also the one who allowed the wastefulness of evolution, with its blind alleys and its competition for limited resources. What are we to make of all that?

I think the only possible solution lies in a variation of the free-will defence, applied to the whole created world. One might call it 'the free-process defence'. In his great act of creation I believe that God allows the physical world to be itself, not in Manichaean opposition to him, but in that independence which is Love's gift of freedom to the one beloved. That world is endowed in its fundamental constitution with an anthropic potentiality which makes it capable of fruitful evolution. The exploration and realization of that potentiality is achieved by the universe through the continual interplay of chance and necessity within its unfolding process. The cosmos is given the opportunity to be itself. I have written of such a world that it is

a world of orderliness but not of clockwork regularity, of potentiality without predictability, endowed with an assurance of development but with a certain openness as to its actual form. It is inevitably a world with ragged edges, where order and disorder interlace each other and where the exploration of possibility by chance will lead not only to the evolution of systems of increasing complexity, but also to the evolution of systems imperfectly formed and malfunctioning.[27]

It is just such a world that W. H. Vanstone describes. He is motivated, not by thoughts arising from science, but from a profound analysis of the vulnerability necessary in the creative gift of love. He writes:

> The activity of God in creation must be precarious. It must proceed by no assured programme. Its progress, like every progress of love, must be an angular progress – in which each step is a precarious step into the unknown.[28]

It is from that precariousness that natural evil arises, for 'The existence of evil must be seen as the expression or consequence of the precariousness of divine creativity'.[29] God no more expressly wills the growth of a cancer than he expressly wills the act of a murderer, but he allows both to happen. He is not the puppetmaster of either men or matter.

When Austin Farrer considered the Lisbon earthquake, which had caused great devastation and loss of life in 1755 and had presented a severe problem of theodicy for eighteenth-century thought, he wrote that: 'The will of God in the event is his will for the elements of the earth's crust or under it: his will that they should go on being themselves and acting in accordance with their natures.'[30] Exactly so. God accords to the processes of the world that same respect that he accords to the actions of humanity. That is why, when we attempted to speak of providence and of miracle, we sought to do so in a way that fully protected cosmic integrity. Our discussion was framed in terms of consistency and not of interference, the discovery of deeper coherence rather than the exhibition of an arbitrary power.

The open flexibility of the world's process affords the means by which the universe explores its own potentiality, humankind exercises its will, and God interacts with his creation. The first, through its limitation and frustration, gives rise to physical evil. The second, through its sinfulness, gives rise to moral evil. The world so marred is not abandoned, for the third is the means by which the Creator can exercise a providential care within the evolving history of his creation.

It remains a question whether the God we are describing is not nevertheless in the end so evacuated of power that he becomes little more than the colluder with cosmic process. John Lucas describes the danger: 'God's plans, it seems, are either vacuous' (he goes along with whatever happens) 'or else the victim of every bloody minded man, and ineffective.'[31] Faced with the dilemma of either a God who withdraws the gift of freedom or a God who is frustrated by the gift of freedom, Lucas opts for the latter as 'the cross on which God has chosen to be impaled . . . It is a corollary of caring; that one should be vulnerable, and a God who cares infinitely will be infinitely vulnerable.'[32]

Lucas's choice of words reminds us of the fundamental Christian insight about God's relation to suffering and evil. He is not a spectator but a fellow-sufferer, who has himself absorbed the full force of evil. In the lonely figure hanging in the darkness and dereliction of Calvary the Christian believes that he sees God opening his arms to embrace the bitterness of the strange world he has made. The God revealed in the vulnerability of the incarnation and in the vulnerability of creation are one. He is the crucified God, whose paradoxical power is perfected in weakness, whose selfchosen symbol is the King reigning from the gallows.

In the end, whatever shift may be made intellectually to grapple with the problem of evil, the only satisfactory conclusion to the matter will come if it is indeed true that 'all shall be well'. That assurance came to Julian of Norwich in the course of her visions of the passion of Christ.[33] The cross is the fundamental basis of Christian theodicy, for in Christ 'all the fullness of God was pleased to dwell, and through him to reconcile to himself all things, whether on earth or in heaven, making peace by the blood of his cross.'[34]

6

Prayer

The practice of prayer is central to religion. It is no accident that the great spiritual autobiography of Augustine's *Confessions* is cast in the form of an extended prayer. Peter Baelz is right to say that 'Prayer is a touchstone of a man's religious beliefs'.[1] Of course, prayer is a complex activity, with many aspects to it. It includes worship, the acknowledgement of the greatness of God. It includes a meditative waiting upon him in stillness and silence. For those who are far advanced in its practice, it will include the contemplative experience of unity with the divine. But for all, it will also include petition, the asking of something from God, for ourselves or for others. Jesus encourages this in the Gospels with an embarrassing directness. 'Ask and it will be given you; seek and you will find; knock and it will be opened to you.'[2] Petition is the form of prayer that relates directly to the issue we are considering in this essay.

One could hardly imagine oneself asking the God of deism for anything. One might well adore him for his mighty act of creation but one could not expect him to do anything about individual happenings within its process. The best one could hope for would be that he had so cleverly constituted his timeless action that things would work out reasonably well. Petitionary prayer implies belief in a God who acts in the particular as well as in the general. We have given reasons why, with appropriate safeguards for creaturely freedom, belief in such a God is a coherent possibility.

But why does he need us to ask him? We cannot suppose that we are informing him of concerns of which he is ignorant, or reminding him of things he had forgotten, or making suggestions he had not thought of, or coercing his reluctant will by magical manipulation. If God is benevolent, will he not give us all that is good without our having continually to ask for it?

Some have seen the answer to lie in ourselves rather than in God.

Prayer is then a donning of the theological 'spectacles behind the eyes' with which we can begin to see what God is actually doing in the world. Aquinas says that 'We must pray, not in order to inform God of our needs and desires, but in order to remind ourselves that in these matters we need divine assistance'[3] and, presumably, that we receive it. On this view, petition becomes a form of disguised meditation on grace, or a kind of spiritual exercise in providential pattern recognition. That it may, and indeed will, have these results is true but I do not think they can be the principal purpose of petitionary prayer. Jesus said 'ask and you will receive', not just 'look and you will see'.

We move closer to the mark with Augustine's comment that 'God does not need to have our will made known to him – he cannot but know it – but he wishes our desire to be exercised in prayer that we may be able to receive what he is preparing to give.'[4] In other words, prayer is neither the manipulation of God nor just the illumination of our perception, but it is the alignment of our wills with his, the correlation of human desire and divine purpose. That alignment is not just a passive acceptance of God's will by human resignation (though 'if it be thy will' is an essential part of any prayer, since God is the necessary partner in it) but it is also a resolute determination to share in the accomplishment of that will (so that prayer is never divorced from action, nor a substitute for it). Prayer is a collaborative personal encounter between man and God, to which both contribute.

The picture that we have been building up in earlier chapters is that of a world of regularity but not of rigidity, within whose evolving history there is room for action initiated both by human will (which we experience directly) and by divine will (which we acknowledge by faith). There must be a delicate balance between structure and flexibility, between the respect for cosmic freedom (which delivers physical process from arbitrary interruption) and the respect for human freedom (which allows us the exercise of choice and responsibility) and the respect for divine freedom (which does not reduce God to the role of an impotent spectator of the history of his creation). It is an immensely difficult task, beyond our powers to accomplish in any detail, to see how this works out, but I claim that the insights of science, and in particular the death of mere mechanism, are consonant with this view. The room for manoeuvre that exists for the

70

accomplishment of divine and human ends through cosmic process, will surely be enhanced by that collaborative alignment of God's will and ours which lies at the heart of petitionary prayer. People have sometimes spoken in a derogatory way of notions of divine action as 'laser beam' interference. Properly understood, the metaphor is a fruitful one. Laser light is characterized by what the physicists call 'coherence', that is to say all the oscillations are in phase, perfectly in step with each other. In that way, effects which otherwise might cancel each other out, can instead afford each other the maximum reinforcement. We can truly use the metaphor of God's laser interaction, not to mean an arbitrarily focused intervention, but as the tuning of divine and human wills to mutual resonance through the collaboration of prayer. The 'laser action' of the virginal conception would result from the complete obedience of Mary's 'Behold, I am the handmaid of the Lord'.[5] Understood in this way it is not inconceivable 'that our asking in faith may make it possible for God to do something that he could not have done without our asking'.[6] In that way prayer is genuinely instrumental. That instrumentality is located neither solely at the divine end (as if it were the result of a change of God's mind) nor at the human end (as if it were a magical demand) but in the personal encounter between God and man by which a new possibility comes into existence. Because of the web of interrelated process of the world, it is not inconceivable that that new possibility can have consequences for a third person, so that prayer for others, as well as ourselves, seems a coherent possibility. Brümmer points out that another consequence of the view of prayer as the vehicle of divine-human co-operation is that 'corporate prayer is more effective than individual prayer, not because it brings more pressure to bear on God, but because it enlists more people in the realization of God's will'.[7]

The co-operation with God involved in prayer is not limited to making available our capacity for action. John Lucas makes an extremely important point when he says:

We are not only, though within limits, the originators of actions, but also, though within limits, the origin of values . . . The mere fact that we want something is a reason, though not a conclusive reason, for God giving it us . . . By creating us and the world he has abdicated not merely absolute sway over the course of events but also absolute sway over the scale of values.[8]

Here is another reason why we have to ask, to commit ourselves to what it is that we desire. The blind man who comes to Jesus has to declare what it is he wants done for him.[9] The encounter of prayer is genuinely two-way; we are not faced by God with an illusion of choice. He is not a celestial Henry Ford, offering us a car of any colour provided it is black. It is an astonishing thought that our preferences should play a part in determining what is to be achieved through creation, but that is part of the loving respect of a Father for his children. Loving respect is due also from children to their Father. One of the reasons why we must seek the coming of God's Kingdom through our prayer is that thereby 'we acknowledge that his perfect goodness (on which we can count) does not exclude his being a person (upon whose free decision we may not presume)'.[10] The necessity for prayer is well summarized by H. D. McDonald when he writes:

> It may indeed be that God does give His best possible to every man without prayer, for He makes his sun to rise on the evil and the good. But the best possible that God, as faithful Creator, assures without prayer to every man may not be the best possible which could come to any man if he really prayed.[11]

Prayer only makes sense within a certain type of universe. The mechanical world of Laplace's calculator, where both past and future are inexorably contained within the dynamical circumstances of the present, would be too rigid a world to have prayer (or humanity, for that matter) within it. We have seen that it is also not the world of modern science (p. 28). Prayer also only makes sense with a certain kind of God. A God totally above the temporal process, with the future as clearly present to him as the past, would be a suspect collaborator in the encounter of prayer. The difficulty was put to Origen by his friend Ambrose, in the clearest terms: 'If God foreknows the future, and if this must needs come to pass, prayer is vain.'[12] We shall return to the question of God's relation to time in the next chapter. Meanwhile, we note that the actual asymmetry between fixed past and open future places a limitation on prayer. It is generally conceded by philosophical theologians that God has no power to change the past. (Once again we encounter the question of the scope of God's action; see p. 31.) The Jewish Rabbis taught that if one hears a fire alarm one is not to pray that the fire is not at one's own house. This is not only because that would be wishing ill on someone else, but also because the fire is where it is. Milton Steinberg sums it up by saying 'a man shall not pray that facts be not facts'.[13] It is a caution against always allowing our instincts to guide our thoughts, to recognize how difficult it is, in the consultant's waiting-room, to follow this logically impeccable injunction.

Our discussion of prayer, like our discussion of miracle, divides into two parts. In the first I have sought to show that prayer is not a nonsensical idea but rather that it is a rational possibility within the world we actually inhabit. Of course many things may be possible which may not actually happen. We have to go on to ask if there are experiential grounds for believing in petitionary prayer.

Since prayer is not magic it will not be testable in a crudely experimental way. If I prayed yesterday that I should receive in the post today an unsolicited cheque for a thousand pounds, its non-arrival does not entitle me to conclude that prayer is a delusion. That remains true for much more serious requests, such as the sustained earnest prayer that someone one loves should be cured of a serious illness. The essence of prayer is that it is not a mechanical operation, predictable in advance, but that it is a personal encounter with God, whose character and outcome are only revealed in the event itself. It is characteristic of all personal encounter that we cannot say beforehand what we shall receive through it. Moreoever, it is only those who participate in the encounter who can afterwards evaluate its content. A friend of mine was mortally ill and was given six months to live. His wife was encouraged by a wise friend to pray with her husband daily and to lay her hands upon him for healing. He died almost exactly six months to the day from the time he had received the news from his doctors. Afterwards his wife asked herself what healing he had received through her prayerful ministry. She concluded that his quiet acceptance of the destiny of imminent death (which profoundly moved many people around him) and the peacefulness of his passing (which might, in view of his disease, have been very distressing) were the healing he had received. Only she could reach that conclusion. Only she could say her prayer was answered, even if the answer might not have been in the form hoped for at the beginning.

Testimony of this kind meets the need expressed by Baelz when he writes:

> If we must be careful of the dangers involved in making an objectively *experimental* issue out of prayer, lest we find ourselves deserting the insights of religion for the delusions of magic, may we not claim there is a discernible *experiential* side to prayer?[14]

Personal experience is irreducibly individual and in consequence its record is inescapably anecdotal. It would be disingenuous not to recognize that a significant part of that record involves cases where apparently unanswered prayer remains a mystery to those who were closely involved. Canon John Gunstone tells of how, in a prayer group, he heard of a woman in her thirties who was suffering from terminal cancer. She lived far away from Manchester, where he worked, and he did not know her. A little later he decided he ought to write to her, but as he began to do so he was seized by the conviction that he did not need to do so because they would meet the next day. He was due to preach at a church forty miles away from where the woman was living. As he sat down to lunch before the service, he asked his host if he knew the woman. He said that he did not but she and her husband had written to him, out of the blue, to ask if it would be permissible for them to come to the Eucharist for healing which was Gunstone's reason for being there. After the service a couple made their way to him. 'Are you Philip and Heather?' he asked. They were astonished to be greeted by name and John Gunstone explained the remarkable sequence of events which had led to their meeting. It seemed that God's hand was in the encounter and Gunstone was moved to say 'Heather, I believe the Lord has arranged this meeting so that we can anoint you and pray for your healing.' She answered that she believed that too. Within three months she was dead. John Gunstone tells us that 'For a long time afterwards I avoided being involved in the ministry of healing. Over and over again I wanted to say with the psalmist "Has God forgotten to be merciful?".'[15]

Peter Baelz presents the challenge: 'Can we, however, discern any coherent moral and spiritual pattern linking the occasions in which God grants a petition with those he refuses?'[16] A general answer seems impossible. Against the deep perplexity of different individual destinies can only be set the infinite variety of individual circumstance and the deep intuition of faith that, all things notwithstanding, God is to be trusted. That insight of faith is most movingly expressed in the Russian Contakion of the Departed:

All we go down to the dust;
and, weeping at the grave, we make our song:
alleluya, alleluya, alleluya.

Although personal experience is a matter for private interpretation, it might be thought that it would have its public aspect in the exhibition of statistically significant trends within sufficiently large populations. After all, that is how the social sciences often seek to operate in analysing the collective effects of individual actions. An early attempt to apply statistical techniques to the evaluation of the efficacy of prayer was made by Sir Francis Galton. He considered royal personages and clergy, as two classes of people most persistently prayed for, and examined the mortality statistics to see if there were discernible beneficial effects. He did not find them. He also drily observed that the insurance offices 'so wakeful to sanitary influence, absolutely ignore prayer as one of them'. His conclusion was to relegate prayer to the category of outmoded superstition.

Various replies are possible. One is to point out that many other factors are at work determining longevity and it is not possible to isolate prayer as the controlling influence on the groups considered. For example, sovereigns were found to be the shortest lived of all those who had access to good nourishment and housing. It has been suggested that, in the nineteenth century, this might have been due to their being most open to the hazards of continual ministrations from the medical profession! But the fundamental answer must be that prayer is human collaboration with God's will and it is not clear that his will coincides with the expectations of eudaemonism, in the simple bestowal of short-term happiness. We return, as inevitably we must, to the mystery of the cross of Christ. Jesus died in his thirties; Paul describes the apostolic life as that of 'men sentenced to death'[17]. It is a preacher's cliché to say that prayer does not deliver us from trouble but preserves us in trouble, but, like most clichés, it is true. The cross provides the only framework in which we shall begin to make sense of the Christian experience of prayer.

7

Time

One of the great discoveries of this century is that the universe itself has a history. We are able to trace its unfolding development from the fiery explosion of the big bang, some fifteen billion years ago. We ourselves are embedded in time. Few distinctions are more fundamental for us than the contrast between the fixity of the past and the uncertainty of the future. How is God related to the temporal flow? If he acts in particular ways upon the world then these actions must take place within its developing process.

Classical theism detaches God from the experience of time. It pictures him surveying the world from an eternal viewpoint, so that Aquinas can say that God does not foreknow the future, he simply knows it. All time is present to him in a simple act of perception. The classic definition of the eternity enjoyed by the timeless God was given by Boethius: 'the complete and perfect possession at once of an endless life'.[1] The key phase is 'at once'. It is the attempt to allow God to be aware of a changing world without subjecting him to change.

In talk of this kind, time is being assimilated to space, so that the complete history of the universe is thought of as laid out on a four-dimensional spacetime 'map' for instant perusal by God. The old-style classical relativists thought of physical process in an exactly similar way. Particles were represented by 'world lines', paths which recorded the sequence of a particle's position as time moved on from start to finish. I say 'moved on', but of course in this way of thinking time is just a parameter labelling successive points along the world line. Time does not elapse; the world line is not traversed. It is simply there. Spacetime diagrams are great chunks of frozen history. Not only can God take an atemporal view of such a universe; it is really the only right perspective from which to consider it. Just before his death Einstein wrote the astonishing words: 'For us convinced physicists, the distinction between past, present and future is an illusion, though a persistent one.'[2]

Such talk is only possible in a totally deterministic universe, where Laplace's calculator can retrodict the past and predict the future from the dynamic circumstances of the present, so that effectively the distinction between past, present and future is abolished. There is simply a given spacetime pattern. That world is a world of being, but it is not a world of becoming. Nothing essentially new can ever happen within it. That world is certainly not the world of human experience, where the past is closed and the future is open. Nor is it the world described by modern science.

In his attitude, Einstein was the last of the great ancients rather than the first of the great moderns. It is notorious that he rejected the radical indeterminism of probabilistic quantum theory. He could not stomach a God who played dice. Yet that is the picture of subatomic process to which almost all physicists subscribe today. In the act of measurement 'the wave packet collapses', that is to say, one of a variety of conceivable outcomes is realized in a manner both unpredictable and radically uncaused. The inability to specify beforehand the result of a quantum measurement implies an openness to the future built into the structure of the world at its constituent roots. In between acts of measurement a quantum mechanical system is represented by a smoothly evolving wave function, which is an expression of potentiality (that is to say, it contains within itself the possibility of various outcomes), rather than the specification of actuality (which would imply a precise and picturable representation of where the system is and what it is doing). Thus quantum theory does not encourage the view that the flux of time is an illusion. Successive acts of measurement bring about genuinely new states of the system.[3]

That demur is reinforced by our modern understanding of the delicate unpredictability of complex dynamical systems (see pp. 28f.). The recognition that mere mechanism is not enough has led to an essential role for becoming in the evolution of the physical world, over and above that required by quantum theory. We recall that Prigogine and Stengers discuss how, if a system has sufficient complexity to include a random element within its behaviour, then

the difference between past and future, and therefore irreversibility, enter into its description . . . The arrow of time [from past to future] is the manifestation oi the fact that the future is not given that, as the French poet Paul Valéry emphasized, 'time is a construction'.[4]

All these considerations emphasize how different time is from space, how seriously we must take its unfolding as a process of genuine becoming. The future is not already formed ahead of us, waiting to reveal itself to our exploration, as the fixed contours of a valley reveal themselves to the traveller who makes his way through them. The future is in part our creation: its shape is responsive to our moulding, as the clay is formed by the sculptor to create his irreducibly new thing, which is his work of art. If even the omnipotent God cannot act to change the past, it does not seem any more conceivable that the omniscient God can know with certainty the unformed future. He may well be able to make highly informed conjectures about its possible shape, he may have prepared his plans for any eventuality, but in his actual experience and knowledge he must be open to the consequences of the exercise of human free will and (as we have suggested earlier, p. 66) the evolution of cosmic free process. God is to be credited with a sort of current omniscience, which Swinburne spells out as meaning: 'P is omniscient if he knows about everything except those future states and their consequences which are not physically necessitated by anything in the past; and if he knows that he does not know about these future states.'[5]

Such a view of God does not at all seem at odds with the biblical account. He is a God active in history and responsive to it. Repentance can avert his judgement and apostasy incur it.[6] When he says 'Behold the former things have come to pass and new things I now declare; before they spring forth I tell you of them',[7] one feels that this is because he is bringing them about, not because he has spied them lying waiting in the future. He is a God described by his acts; the One who brought Israel out of Egypt and raised Jesus from the dead. He is a God who responds to the prayers of his people. Abraham's pleading for Sodom and Gomorrah[8] is not a charade about an already determined future (cf p. 72). The God who simply surveys spacetime from an eternal viewpoint is the God of deism, whose unitary act is that frozen pattern of being. Karl Barth says of the Christian God that:

'Without God's complete temporality the content of the Christian message has no shape.'[9] That is because the Christian gospel is an unfolding drama of redemption, not a timeless moment of illumination.

The school in contemporary theology which has taken the temporal aspect of God most seriously is process theology. Colin Gunton says of its chief proponent, Charles Hartshorne, that the key to his thought lies in its stress on the subjectivity of God, with the understanding that it is the subjective knower who is affected by his knowledge, rather than the one known.[10] (Actually, reflection both on interpersonal encounter and on quantum measurement would encourage a more reciprocal view of the act of knowing.) Such a subjective God is embedded in time, but he is in danger of being in thrall to time. Hartshorne sought to safeguard against this through the idea of a dipolar God, who has both necessary existence and contingent actuality – who enjoys both eternity and temporality. God's dipolarity means that he is 'absolute perfection in *some* respects, relative perfection in others'.[11] An example of relative perfection would be the current omniscience we spoke about earlier.

There is great attraction in the notion of divine dipolarity, which offers us the God of both being and becoming, the reconciliation, one might say, of the God of the philosophers and the God of the Bible. Certainly, divine temporality, provided it is balanced by divine eternity, would be no mark of imperfection. Peter Baelz summarizes well the theological necessity that there should be 'both an eternal fount of love and a continuing expression of love'.[12] It is more open to question whether the particular synthesis that Hartshorne proposes achieves the necessary balance. Gunton says that Hartshorne's God 'is essentially not pure being but pure becoming',[13] a view which seems endorsed when we note Hartshorne's contention that 'becoming is reality itself, and being only an aspect of this reality'.[14] The event-dominated metaphysic of Whitehead is almost bound to lead to such a lopsided stance.

While it is true that the God of becoming is needed if God is to be responsive to his evolving and suffering creation, it is also true that the God of being is needed if he is to be the guarantor of the order of creation and the ground of its hope. The modern scientific view of the universe, with its reliable underlying law but flexible open process,[15] offers encouragement to the search for a dipolar God who is the source of the world's lawfulness and who interacts with its process. Keith Ward has sought to give an account of a God 'internally complex' which is closer to orthodox theology than process theology succeeds in being.[16] He says of his attempt that: 'Once one accepts the idea of a temporal, everlasting God, one is committed to explaining the finite world, partly as governed in its existence and structure by his necessary nature, and partly expressing his freely chosen purpose.'[17] Such a God can be both the God whose reason underlies the marvellous rational transparency of the physical world, open to human inquiry, and also the God who is not condemned merely to contemplating or guaranteeing that world's regularity, but who is also able to exercise his will within it. God's *chesed*, his steadfast love, requires, not fixity of experience (which is the negation of responding love) but unchangeable benevolence of will (which is the way in which he is steadfast). He does not need that protection from involvement upon which Farrer insisted when he said 'God has no history; what is done in history through the action of his will is done by, and happens to, his creation'.[18] Yet he is not to become so enmeshed in the flux of the world that Christian theology becomes, as Gunton says process theology has been described as being, 'a sophisticated form of animism'.[19] The dipolar God is really exhibiting one aspect of the long-recognized duality of God's transcendance (his kingly rule from above) and his immanence (his working from within). The true God is neither a detached tyrant nor a pantheistic influence; he is at once 'the high and lofty one who inhabits eternity' and at the same time the one who dwells 'with him who is of a contrite and humble spirit'.[20] Religious experience has always had to hold these fundamental intuitions in tension with each other. They are part of the dialectic of divine eternity and divine temporality.

There is one difficulty which all talk of time within God must face. It is the question, which time? The theory of special relativity abolished the Newtonian idea, seemingly so congenial to our everyday experience, of one, uniformly flowing, universal time. It replaced it by a multitude of individual times experienced by different observers, according to their different states of motion. Moving clocks run slow, and the twin who is shot off in the spacecraft returns to Earth to find his brother grown much older than he is. Gunton was aware of the problem this posed for talk about God's temporal experience.[21] What clock does he use? I do not believe that this is an insuperable difficulty, though the answer must be mildly technical. We can picture each observer's 'instant' as being a three-dimensional slice through four-dimensional spacetime. Events in this slice are simultaneous as far as that observer is concerned, but because different observers take differently oriented slices, they do not agree among themselves about the meaning of simultaneity. However, as an observer's temporal experience unfolds his 'slices' move through spacetime, in due course sweeping out the whole. An *omnipresent* observer, whose direct contact with the way things are is not located at a point within the slice but spread out all over it, would in due course experience everywhere and everywhen. That would be true whatever his choice of time axis. In the case of the twins, for example, suppose that the omnipresent God's time coincides with that of the one left on Earth. Then the divine clock would not be 'ticking' at the same rate as that of the twin in the spacecraft but, because God is everywhere present, he experiences all that happens to that twin *as it happens*, just as he does for the one left on Earth. Two spatially coincident observers can agree on 'now' because, however they choose to label it, they are at that instant at the same spacetime point. The omnipresent God has no need to use signalling to tell him what is happening and so he has instant access to every event as and when it occurs. That totality of experience is presumably the most important thing to be able to say about God's relation to world history. He would not miss anything and his action would always be causally coherent, since it is an essential property of relativity that causal relationships are independent of the choice of temporal reference frame. (In this respect there is as much absolutism as relativity in the theory.)

Finally, there is in fact a natural time to use in speaking of God's experience of creation. It is cosmic time, defined with respect to the overall structure of the world, that natural frame of reference that cosmologists use when speaking of the current age of the universe. (In an expanding, homogeneous universe, such as we inhabit, the density of matter (averaged over many galaxies), or the temperature of the background radiation, provide a natural measure of the current age.) So I do not think that talk of temporality in God is made incoherent by relativity.

Nor is it incoherent, in my view, to believe that the temporal aspect of God had a beginning. That is just one of the implications that follow from the act of creation by which both the world and time were brought into being by him. Of course, God himself did not come into being then, for in his eternity he is the One who is. God is love from all eternity to all eternity, but his Creatorly love finds its expression in the temporally evolving act of creation. We do not need to follow Aquinas in thinking of God as *actus purus*, all actuality, without the possibility of development, provided we are able to conceive of a dynamical idea of perfection, in which change takes place without diminution, rather than perfection being the retaining of a frozen eminence. There is no 'best moment' in a great work of music, on which our ears should seek to linger for ever; the beauty lies in the unfolding pattern of the whole movement. God's perfection is not the static holding of the topmost metaphysical peak, but it lies in the total love of his unfailing action. It is the perfection that belongs to life and not to lifelessness. That is, perhaps, easier for us to grasp now that we know that the act of creation was no production of a ready-made world, but the letting-be of cosmic evolution, from big bang to present day. God shows himself to be the One who works by unfolding process, and surely there must be within himself a developing, but always perfectly appropriate, relation to what comes to be.

There is a surprising tendency in modern theological thought to espouse the idea that the universe must be everlasting. It is a natural hazard for those inclined to the notion of divine embodiment (p. 20), but we also find it in process theology[22] and, more surprisingly, in Farrer: 'Since it is nonsensical to suppose a beginning of the Creator, we shall take it that he has always been creatively engaged upon material realities; the physical world has always been.'[23] The self-confidence of metaphysicians is sometimes breathtaking. It is, of course, nonsensical to suppose a beginning of God, but not of his Creatorly relation to the world. A God who is not *actus purus* does not have to be everything possible 'at once'. Unless we believe that this really is the best possible world (p. 64), we have to recognize this in any case, since he has in fact created this universe rather than another which might have been equally suitable. Scientifically, all that we can say about the matter is that we have no reason to suppose the universe to have existed prior to the big bang, though there are highly speculative extrapolations before that which just might make sense (p. 29).

The final question one must ask about God's involvement in time is whether it deprives him of his sovereignty over his creation. If he is reacting to events, is he not the servant rather than the master? Vernon White protests against this when he says that: 'Consequent will [that is to say, the acceptance of occurrence, which we called "acquiescent will" (p. 7)] implies circumstances beyond control, which is precisely what cannot be predicated of an almighty Creator God.'[24] We have already said that creation involves a kenosis, an acceptance by God of the precariousness necessary in his enterprise of giving freedom to creation (pp. 66f.). This should not be surprising to a religion, one of whose central acts of revelation is the *passion* of Christ. It is the necessary costliness of love, for 'where love is, action is destined to pass into passion: working into waiting'.[25] But what is beyond total control is not beyond total redemption.

Maurice Wiles offers us a model of creation as an improvised drama:

> In the process of getting deeper into their parts and discovering their reactions to one another in the given situation, they may be led on to enact a kind of drama which the author had always intended and already envisaged in principle though not in detail. The resultant drama would be both the author's and the actors', though we would be more ready to speak of the author as agent of the drama as a whole than as agent of any of the individual speeches or incidents within it.[26]

The last sentence expresses Wiles's deistic 'single action' view of God's activity. I would want to modify the image, not by turning creation into puppet theatre with God pulling the strings, nor by his occasional intervention as a powerful but invisible actor, but rather (if the metaphor will bear it) by his being producer as well as author, in continual relationship with the actors in the unfolding drama. And, of course, it is Christian belief that in Christ he has also appeared on the stage as one of the visible actors. We cannot leave the question of God's action in the world without some attempt to consider the doctrine of the incarnation.

8

Incarnation and Sacrament

Christian belief speaks of two very specific modes of God's interaction with the world. One is the incarnation, the Christian claim that God has actually lived the life of a man in Jesus Christ. The other is the concept of sacrament, the claim that such ordinary substances as bread and wine and water participate in some way in the communication of divine grace. These are tremendous assertions and any adequate discussion of them calls for extensive treatment. This chapter cannot be more than a brief interlude in which to explore whether there is any consonance between these claims and the general account of God's relation to the world and its process which we are pursuing in this essay. The discussion can be no more than a crude identification of themes, whose proper exploration would call for a book in itself.

Our view may be summarized as being expressed in a complementary metaphysic where human participation in a noetic world arises from mind being the complementary pole of matter in flexible open organization.[1] Such a scheme accommodates our basic experiences of reasoning and choice, without denying the essential reality of our physical embodiment. Just as it allows us to act in the world, so it also makes coherent the possibility that God is in a relationship with his creation which goes beyond his simply being the upholder of its order. It allows for the exercise of his providential care within the unpredictable unfolding of world history. We must go on first to ask whether it is also a world-view within which incarnation has a credible place.

An account of God's action in the world which confined him to a single deistic letting-be would scarcely be adequate for that task. Incarnation would then either be ruled out altogether, or else become so totally singular an instance as to be rendered incredible. If God became man in Jesus that must, of course, be a unique event, but it must also bear some coherent relationship to the course of events in which it was embedded. Otherwise it would be a docetic charade. Maurice Wiles would then be right to say that it would distance 'Jesus from the rest of history in the kind of way that led Marcion to see him as the emissary of some higher God, other than the creator'.[2] The general theological insight that grace completes nature, rather than supplanting it, must be true of the particular and intensified case of the incarnation. It is the same God who is known as Creator and Redeemer. Therefore I think that David Brown is right to say that 'belief or non-belief in an interventionist God is integral to the question of what will be said about the nature of any possible incarnation',[3] except that I would want to replace the fitful word 'interventionist' by the reliable word 'interacting'.

The incarnation must be at once continuous and discontinuous – discontinuous because it is a new act of God; continuous because it takes place within the evolving history of humanity. The virginal conception is a symbol (in my view, a historically acted symbol) of the discontinuity of God's initiative and the continuity of human participation through the obedience of Mary.

The New Testament account of Christ is dominated by the conviction that in Jesus is encountered a great act of salvation for humankind. Any reckoning of who he was must be adequate to explain how Jesus came to be known as Saviour, the source of new life and new hope. Therefore I believe that Maurice Wiles is mistaken to take the view that 'there is no difference in kind as far as God's action in the world is concerned between the case of Jesus and the case of other human persons'.[4] That assertion runs counter to actual Christian experience. Wiles believes that it is necessary in order to safeguard the genuine humanity of Jesus. I want to safeguard that humanity, but I also want to safeguard the Church's experience that 'if anyone is in Christ, he is a new creation; the old has passed away, behold the new has come'.[5] From the earliest times there has been this testimony to encounter with a particular and unique saving action of God in Christ. Its understanding will be no easy matter, but it is common experience, in science as well as religion, that reality is subtle beyond our powers of prior expectation. I have argued elsewhere that the necessity to do justice to Christian experience will lead us to struggle with the mystery that in Christ we encounter the human and the divine.[6]

Since the noetic world of a complementary metaphysic is a created world, which does not contain God himself within it,[7] the principal picture on which this essay is based will not, of itself, serve to provide direct help for us in that struggle. There is an inevitable ineffability, limiting us finite creatures in our attempts to describe how the infinite God could be focused on the finite man Jesus, in such a way that it is possible to say of him that he is wholly divine (*totus deus*), though not, of course, the whole of the divine (*totum dei*). Yet it does seem to me that the dipolar picture of God, advocated in Chapter 7, when combined with Trinitarian insight to suggest something of the richness of the divine nature, can afford some help in considering a kenotic model for the incarnation.[8] In David Brown's words, the latter pictures 'the divine reality literally abandoning its characteristic divine powers and thus experiencing a *kenosis* of self-emptying which reduces it to a human nature, initially no more than a foetus'.[9] The extreme difficulty of such an idea is expressed by one of its modern proponents, John Austin Baker, when he writes: 'we find ourselves bewildered by the notion of a single person existing at once within the terms of the created order and also being continuously present to that order as its Creator.'[10]

Trinitarianism and dipolarity both suggest something of the complexity of the divine nature, and it is surely necessary to combine their insights in our feeble efforts to speak of God. Each of the divine Persons is to be conceived as possessing his eternal and his temporal pole. It will be the *temporal* pole of the Son which is involved in the kenotic focusing of the infinite upon the finite, in the *historical* episode of the incarnation. The temporal poles of the Father and the Spirit would continue God's rule over the general process of the world and his immanent working within it, without any suspension of divine providence in the early years of the first century. By their characters, the eternal poles of all the divine Persons remain unchanging and unchanged. Dimly one perceives that in such a way one might hope to satisfy Charles Gore's demand that we should conceive that: 'In some manner the humiliation and self-limitation of the incarnate state was compatible with the continual exercise of divine and cosmic functions in another sphere.'[11] At the same time, a Nestorian division between divine impassibility and human vulnerability is overcome, since the temporal pole is precisely God in relation to, and affected by, what is happening.

It is clear that we are appealing to a much more 'social' picture of the divine Trinity than that encouraged by the 'Christian monotheism' which has been the classical stance of Western theology. Jürgen Moltmann has been a vigorous defender of such a social approach.[12] It is also characteristic of his thought to link Trinitarianism with the history of Jesus Christ, giving the discussion a thoroughgoing temporal aspect. Concerning the cry of dereliction from the cross, he writes:

> If we take the relinquishment of the Father's name in Jesus' death cry seriously, then this is even the breakdown of the relationship that constitutes the very life of the Trinity: if the Father forsakes the Son, the Son does not merely lose his sonship. The Father loses his fatherhood as well. The love that binds the one to the other is transformed into a dividing curse. It is only as the One who is forsaken and cursed that the Son is still the Son. It is only as the One who forsakes, who surrenders the other, that the Father is still present. Communicating love and responding love are alike transformed into infinite pain and into the suffering and endurance of death.[13]

Later he says that: 'A theological doctrine of the Trinity can only be biblically justified if the *history* of God to which the Bible testifies, itself displays trinitarian forms.'[14] Such emphatic (and biblical) enmeshing of the Trinity and history can only make sense if we attribute a temporal pole to the divine nature.

While the incarnation necessarily remains a mystery, some of its consequences may be examined in the light of our arguments. The resurrection is not a sufficient condition for the truth of the incarnation, but it is surely a necessary one. An incarnated God who died and remained dead would be a contradiction. The resurrection necessarily poses problems for the deist. Maurice Wiles wishes to avoid any special claims, for 'one action of so distinctly different a kind would be sufficient to call in question the claim that the absence of divine intervention in relation to so many evils and disasters in the world is because such direct action is logically incompatible with the kind of world God has chosen to create'.[15] I have acknowledged the problem of why God does not act overtly on so many occasions that seem to call out for divine intervention, but I have suggested that the actual answer lies in the delicate character of the circumstance necessary for such action to be available to a God who respects the freedom of his creation, whilst not being rendered totally impotent to act within its flexible process (p. 33). The perfect alignment of divine and human will in Jesus created a unique regime which may consistently be supposed to have resulted in unique phenomena.

One can go on to say that, if man is truly a matter/mind amphibian, then a man who came alive without a body would be a contradiction. His new body does not have to be made of the same stuff as his old body, but body of some sort he will have to have if he is to remain truly human. On this view, when we come to talk of the hope given to all humankind in Christ, we are not talking about spiritual survival but about resurrection, the reconstitution of the psychosomatic being, even if the new body is a glorified one, as Paul's phrase 'a spiritual body' (*soma pneumatikon*) suggests.[16] Christ's empty tomb would testify to this necessity and, by its symbolism of the Lord's risen body being a transmutation of his dead body, it would also signify that continuity in discontinuity which, for ourselves, Paul declares in his metaphorical talk of seed sowing: 'What you sow is not the body to be but a bare kernel . . . What is sown is perishable, what is raised is imperishable.'[17] In the case of seeds it is the information-carrying DNA which is the link between one generation and the next. Analogously, that immense complexity of information-bearing pattern, which is the real person enduring through all the changes of actual material make-up of our bodies, could be remembered by God and resurrected in that unimaginable new environment of his choosing. It would not be altogether inappropriate to describe our present bodies as 'earthly tents' and to look forward to the hope of 'a building from God, a house not made with hands, eternal in the heavens'.[18] Though the language of Paul in 2 Corinthinians sometimes sounds more like a doctrine of immortality than of resurrection, yet embodiment is retained as ultimately necessary, even if he may have envisaged a period of disembodiment between death and the final consummation. Thus he says that we 'long to put on our heavenly dwelling, so that by putting it on we may not be found naked'.[19] Paul had the Hebrew horror of the 'naked soul' (the life of shades in Sheol), in contrast to the Hellenistic desire for such a purified state, thought to be superior to fleshly encumbrance. Since, like Aristotle, I believe that the soul is the form of the body, not a special spiritual substance contained within it, I do not believe in naked souls, except as remembrances of pattern in the mind of God. The real destiny beyond death for all of us will begin when that pattern which is us is reconstituted in the act of resurrection. It may be that the time of that new world bears no relation to the time of this world and that we pass to experience of it directly at death. Or it may be that that time will only begin to run when this world's process will have been concluded by some great act of God, so that the new world comes into being by the transformation of the old. In that case the dead await their resurrection. Who can say? The Christian belief that Christ's tomb was empty, and that the Lord's risen body is a glorified transmutation of his dead body would most naturally mean that our risen bodies are to be provided by an ultimate redemptive transmutation of the matter of this world, of which Jesus' resurrection was an anticipation. Yet the appearance and disappearance of the risen Lord, followed by his withdrawal from history in the great symbolic act of the ascension, is most naturally interpreted by saying that the two times, of this world and the next, are independent, intersecting only in the appearances of the risen Christ, the resurrection being a transition from one to the other and the empty tomb arising from the 'transfer' of matter from one state to the other. Our talk is more speculative, even, than that of cosmologists assuring us that they know what happened when the universe was less than 10^{-30} seconds old. The only certainty is God himself. Our ultimate hope rests in that faithfulness which will not abandon anything of value once it has come to be.

If it is true, as the Athanasian Creed tells us, that in Christ we see 'the taking of manhood into God', then that taking will have to partake of embodiment, if embodiment is essential to humanity. A simple divine remembrance of having been human will not be an adequate account of what this means. There must be a continuing true humanity contained within the temporal pole of the Son. The language of Article IV of the Church of England's *Articles of Religion*:

Christ did truly rise again from death and took again his body, with flesh, bones and all things pertaining to the perfection of Man's nature; wherewith he ascended into Heaven, and there sitteth until he return to judge all Men at the last day

may seem crude, and even offensive, to our ears. It sees things solely in terms of presently perceived possibility and so it fails to take account of Paul's warning that 'flesh and blood cannot inherit the Kingdom of God, nor does the perishable inherit the imperishable'.[20] Yet the Article's basic intuition, that risen Christ is for ever an embodied Christ, must be correct, even if the form of that embodiment may be wholly different from what we can readily imagine. It may even be that the very strong terms in which Paul speaks of the Christian community as being the body of Christ[21], may be of some relevance. We have rejected the idea of the embodiment of God (the *totum dei*) in his world. It does not follow that we have to reject any notion of the evolving embodiment of Christ, the projection on to the human of the temporal pole of the Son (*totus deus*), in the redeemed community of men and women. Nor, if there are other forms of self-conscious life in the universe, equally in need of redemption as humankind has proved to be, need we have difficulty in supposing that the Second Person of the Trinity would, in his temporal pole, have taken upon himself their nature, and drawn that nature into the Godhead in an act of redemption, thus finding a partial embodiment in them also. If these ideas make any sense at all, it is because they seek to speak in terms of Christ, conceived as the projection of the temporal pole of the Infinite upon the created world of the finite, rather than in terms of the ineffable life of the Second Person. Such a distinction is difficult, and perhaps dangerous, but it seems an inescapable necessity for christological thought that does not take a purely spiritual view of reality. The more seriously one takes the divinity of Christ, the more seriously one must wrestle with the notion that the hypostatic union of his two natures must involve something like the way in which an infinite-dimensional sphere would intersect a two-dimensional plane in the perfect symmetry of a circle. Then, if on other planets there are other created natures united to the Word, that would involve other 'sections' of that divine infinite sphere. The crudeness of this talk

91

would not be removed by attempting lengthy refinement of its language, for it arises from ignorance. The only claim of this discussion upon anyone's attention lies in the attempt to see, with some honesty if limited perspicacity, what it could begin to mean to speak of God as incarnate in irreducibly embodied humanity.

In some ways the mystery of sacrament is even more difficult to fathom, for here we appear to lose direct appeal to the mystery of human personality and instead we are concerned with very ordinary material things, such as bread and wine. I take it that we are dealing neither with magical elements (as St Ignatius' unfortunate phrase describing the Eucharist as 'the medicine of immortality' might almost have seemed to suggest[22]) nor simply with symbolic elements which stir up suitable thoughts by time-honoured association. Neither extreme coincides with the Christian experience that the Eucharist is a real presence of Christ in a way most perplexing but undeniable. Testimony to the real presence is by no means confined to the Catholic and Orthodox traditions alone; it is to be found, for example, in Luther and Calvin,[23] and it has been a continuing tradition within Anglicanism also. Our complementary linking of the noetic and the material might at first sight seem well suited to a sacramental view of the universe, in which the material is perceived as the carrier of the spiritual.[24] The problem, however, is to identify the means by which the association is made and to see if this casts light on sacramental experience.

The medieval doctrine of transubstantiation was a brilliant attempt to deal with this problem in terms of the substance which was held to underlie the accidents of material composition, so that the former became in the sacrament the body and blood of Christ, while the latter remained unchanged. Unfortunately that metaphysical scheme of substance and accidents no longer seems persuasive.

Our complementary metaphysic certainly does not afford a lodging for the idea of substance. The linkage of the noetic with the material lies in the openness of material organization. God's particular action in the world is specifically located in domains where there is flexible process. That does not seem to relate directly to the bread and wine of the Eucharist, whose physical pattern can scarcely be expected to be altered by the Prayer of Thanksgiving. The crude challenge to submit the consecrated elements to physical and chemical analysis would surely not reveal a phase change in the way in which the matter composing them was organized.

If we retain a concentration upon the consecrated elements alone, then we seem faced with an impasse in reconciling Christian experience with the point of view we are maintaining. However, modern Eucharistic thought places emphasis not solely on the elements, but rather upon the whole Eucharistic action, taking place in the gathered community of believers. There is a recovered recognition of the work of the Spirit, who may indeed be thought immanently to act within the openness of the Christian community. Within this wider view we are given a picture of God's action in the sacrament, consistent with what we have been saying about his particular action in the flexible process of the world.

The first Anglican-Roman Catholic International Commission, commenting on the statement that the bread and wine become the body and blood of Christ, says:

> *Becoming* does not imply material change. Nor does the liturgical use of the word imply that the bread and wine become Christ's body and blood in such a way that in the eucharistic celebration his presence is limited to the consecrated elements. It does not imply that Christ becomes present in the eucharist in the same manner that he was present in his earthly life. It does not imply that this *becoming* follows the physical laws of this world.[25]

(I would want to say, however, that the becoming will respect the physical laws ordained by the Creator.) The Commission's Report goes on to say:

> The ultimate change intended by God is the transformation of human beings into the likeness of Christ. The bread and wine *become* the sacramental body and blood of Christ in order that the Christian community may *become* more truly what it already is, the body of Christ.[26]

One thinks of the words of St Augustine in one of his sermons: 'You are the body of Christ and its members; it is your own mystery which lies there on the Lord's table. It is your own mystery which you receive. . . . Be what you see; receive what you are.'

This way of thinking about Christ's sacramental presence seems consistent with what we have been trying to articulate, the collective openness of the worshippers and their gifts to the presence of Christ, which does not reduce merely to the sum of individual thoughts triggered by symbolic action. It is related to what has been said above about the evolving embodiment of Christ in the redeemed community. Our present sacramental experience can be seen as a foretaste and earnest of that ultimate consummation in which 'Christ is all in all'.[27] Gerald O'Collins sees this as the beginning of the outworking of the transforming destiny wrought by the resurrection for the whole of creation. For him, its consequences are not limited to humankind alone and he says that 'the Eucharist provides the supreme example of how the resurrection has already changed the created world'.[28]

In some manner the bread and wine are an integral part of that whole Eucharistic action in a way neither detachably magical nor dispensably symbolic.

Finally, we can note that the line of thought here pursued is readily applied to baptism, the other great sacrament of the gospel, where the participation of the baptized and their sponsors has always been acknowledged as essential to the action.

The incarnation and the sacraments lie at the heart of Christian experience. The purpose of this chapter has been to suggest that they are not foreign to the understanding of God's action in the world that we have been building up in this book. They do not lose their character as Christian mysteries, but they do not appear as irrational surds in the world's process. And of course, ignorance of exactly how something comes about is no reason for denying the experience that it actually happens.

9

Hope

When we survey the physical process of the world, we not only examine the present and reconstruct the past; we can also peer into the future. The history of the universe, on the largest scale, has been that of a continuing tug-of-war between the expansive effect of the fiery explosion of the big bang and the contractive effect of the force of gravity. They are evenly balanced, and our observations are not sufficiently accurate to enable us to predict which will win in the end. Therefore, two possible scenarios are to be envisaged. If expansion wins, the galaxies will condense into black holes which eventually will decay, by one process or another, into degraded states. If, on the other hand, contraction wins, the present expansion will, after many thousands of millions of years, be halted and reversed. The galaxies will then begin to fly together again. What began with the big bang will eventually end with the big crunch, as the whole world collapses into a singular cosmic melting-pot. These two contrasting possibilities happen, respectively, if the universe is what cosmologists call 'open' or 'closed'.

Either way the prospect looks bleak. However, it is possible that even a universe with a finite lifetime (the closed case) can in some sense accommodate infinite experience, and even a decaying universe (the open case) does not degrade so quickly as to preclude this either. Barrow and Tipler have given a careful discussion of these options.[1] They define life as a computer-like capacity for information-processing and storage. One can make use of their arguments without subscribing to so reductionist a point of view, since such a capacity is surely a necessary condition for life, even if one may doubt its sufficiency. They define a Final Anthropic Principle (FAP), requiring that intelligent information-processing must continue to exist 'for ever', meaning by that that the future history of the universe must be compatible with the processing and storage of an infinite number of 'bits' of information. Their conclusion is that, provided matter has certain properties relating to the spectra of particles (properties whose truth or falsehood is at present an open question), then it would be possible to fulfil the Final Anthropic Principle in a closed universe. They are not hopeful about the open case.

Their arguments are essentially thermodynamic in character and relate to very general considerations linking information-processing and storage to energy requirements. Barrow and Tipler distinguish between physical time, measuring the age of the universe, and a kind of cosmic 'psychological' time which measures the rate at which information is being processed. The latter time can turn out to be infinite in span even when the former time is finite. As the universe entered either the very high temperature regimes of the collapsing, closed, universe, or the degraded plasma regimes of the decaying, open, universe, 'life' would cease to take its familiar carbon-based form. It would have to become increasingly exotic in its mode of embodiment, employing the hypothetical physical states required for FAP. The contrivance of these new forms of information-bearing matter is assumed to be brought about as 'intelligence' exerts itself to retain its foothold in changing cosmic circumstances. The 'physical eschatology' of Barrow and Tipler represents the possible continuation of information-laden pattern by means of ever more bizarre types of embodiment. 'An intelligent programme can in principle be run on many types of hardware.'[2] In a curious way the FAP scenario offers hope for 'intelligence' within cosmic history in a way bearing some analogy to the way in which the Christian idea of resurrection offers hope for individuals beyond history (p. 89). The difference between them, however, is striking. FAP offers at best the prospect of endlessly accumulating information. It is a hope bleaker even than those centred on the future of the Race or the Party. Christianity offers the hope of a destiny beyond death for the *individual*. I do not think that either an infinitely accelerating sequence of information-processing events in a collapsing universe, or a never exhausted sequence of such events in a decaying universe, represents sufficient fulfilment of cosmic process to deny the charge that the physical universe as we know it is ultimately condemned to futility. To think otherwise would indeed be 'to sacrifice the individual on the altar of a cosmic plan'.

Ultimate hope, therefore, can be grounded in God alone. Only he is the one in whom 'what is mortal is swallowed up in life'[3] and through whom 'the creation itself will be set free from its bondage to decay and obtain the glorious liberty of the children of God'.[4] But Christian hope is not solely eschatological hope – and so always in danger of becoming pie in the sky – but it must also include hope within the process of the world itself. The fulfilment of God's intentions cannot wait only on a final act by which all things are made new. To suppose that would be to turn God into a God of magic and to deny our knowledge of the God of process patiently at work in his creation. There must be an interim hope as well as a final hope, for the new creation has already begun in Christ.[5] There must be assurance that God's intentions will not be thwarted by the resistance of humanity. Even someone as impressed by the necessary precariousness of creation as Vanstone is, can express firm hope in the God at work within that creation:

> If the creation is the work of love, its 'security' lies not in its conformity to some predetermined plan but in the unsparing love which will not abandon a single fragment of it and man's assurance must be the assurance not that all that happens is determined by God's plan but that all that happens is encompassed by His love.[6]

The clue to the nature of our *present* hope lies exactly in God's continuing interaction with the world that he has made. Only if that interaction is possible is current hope itself a possibility. Surveying the sweep of biological evolution, Arthur Peacocke says that it seems to speak of a Creator who is 'an Improviser of unsurpassed ingenuity.'[7] Hope does not lie in the unfolding of an inexorable plan, ordained by the God of necessity alone and foreseen and calculated in every detail, but it lies in the evolving potentiality of a universe in which chance and necessity maintain their fruitful interplay and within whose open process the immanent activity of God is at work. Despite the role of chance, it is possible for such a universe to contain within its history purposed fulfilments, such as the coming-to-be of self-conscious beings might be held to be, even if the paths by which those fulfilments are attained depend on contingent circumstance. David Bartholomew has given a careful discussion of the ways in which 'chance can lead to certainty', a determined end be reached by an indeterminate path.[8]

This is just one example of the way in which order can arise out of chaos (p. 29). The notion accords with a metaphor offered by P. T. Geach for God's purposeful action in the world, based on the game of chess:

> God and man alike play in the great game. And God is the supreme Grand Master who has everything under his control . . . God, like some grand master of chess, can carry out his plan even if he has announced it beforehand. 'On that square', says the Grand Master, 'I will promote my pawn to queen and deliver checkmate to my adversary'; and it is even so.[9]

I think Geach overstates the case, for he makes God's control too tight. Indeed he believes that God knows the future by controlling it. He goes on to say: 'No line of play that finite players may think of can force God to improvise', and we are dangerously close to a God who is unaffected by his creatures. I would prefer to think of a God who does indeed improvise in response to his creatures' free actions, but who is not ultimately thwarted by them. We have already rejected the idea of a unique 'best possible world'; we may also question the idea of a unique 'best possible route to fulfilment'. But fulfilment there will be. God may not fix his will on delivering checkmate by promoting that pawn on that square, but he will certainly win the game. John Lucas speaks of God and his infinite resource. 'One plan may fail but there are always others. As fast as we torpedo his best design for us, he produces out of his agonized reappraisal a second best.'[10] Or, I would say, an equal good or even – *O felix culpa!* – a better. The infinite God is a source of inexhaustible hope, both within the process of this world and beyond it. Paul's meditation in Romans 9–11 on God's purpose for his ancient people the Jews, following their rejection of the Messiah, illustrates his understanding of such divine resourcefulness. God is not thwarted, for 'if their rejection means the reconciliation of the world, what will their [eventual] acceptance mean but life from the dead?'[11]

Our task has been to suggest that a hope based on a God who can interact with his world in ways more particular than just the general willing of its existence, is a hope which is a coherent possibility within the framework provided by the scientific understanding of cosmic

98

process. This book is far from solving all the many problems involved in trying to understand the nature of God's action, and of our own, but the view it presents encourages the belief that there is a compatibility between the insights of science and the insights of religion. We do not have to choose between the God of the Bible and the God revealed in the pattern and structure of the physical world. A clockwork world of mere mechanism could only be the endlessly spinning system kept in place by the God of deism. The world in fact discerned by modern science has an openness in its becoming which is consonant, not only with its being a world of which we are actually inhabitants, but also a world which is the creation of the true and living God, continually at work within its process.

NOTES

Chapter 1 The Problem

1 See, for example, Davies (1983), Montefiore (1985), Peacocke (1979), Polkinghorne (1986), and even Hoyle (1983).

2 Dukas and Hoffman (1979), p. 43.

3 Kasper (1984), p. 24.

4 For example, Ps. 107, 33–8.

5 Wiles (1986), p. 93.

6 ibid.

7 Davies (1983), p. 208.

8 Wiles (1986), p. 28.

9 Brown (1985), p. 16.

10 See Prestige (1936), p. 63.

11 Job 1.6–12; 2.1–6.

12 Polkinghorne (1988), ch. 4; see also Vanstone (1977).

13 Lucas (1976), p. 9. Wiles (1986, p. 66) comments: 'It is perhaps somewhat rash to assert what no theist would deny.'

14 Brümmer (1984), p. 92.

15 Prestige (1936), ch, 3.

16 Quoted by Farmer (1935), p. 173.

17 See, for example, Hooykaas (1972), Russell (1985).

18 Bryant (1983), pp. 40–41.

19 Baelz (1968), p. 113.

20 Science only appears adequate if reality is treated in a reductionist fashion. For arguments against reductionism, see, for example, Peacocke (1979), ch. 4; Polkinghorne (1986), ch. 6.

21 Rev. 11.17.

22 Gardner (1983), pp. 239–40.

23 Quoted in Wiles (1986), pp. 31–2.

24 Peacocke (1986).

25 Farrer (1967), pp. 65–6.

26 ibid., p. 62.

27 ibid., p. 140.
28 Lucas (1976), p. 7.
29 Farrer (1967), p. 81.
30 Wiles (1986), p. 7.
31 See, for example, Cobb and Griffin (1976).
32 Gunton (1978), p. 223.
33 Ward (1982), p. 229.
34 See, for example, Polkinghorne (1984).
35 Peacocke (1979), p. 132.
36 See, for example, Peacocke (1979), pp. 96-7, and the writings of the process theologians.
37 Moltmann (1981), p. 107.
38 White (1985), p. 91.
39 ibid, p. 7.
40 Pailin (1986), p. 225.
41 See note 6.
42 Ramsey (1973), p. 57.

Chapter 2 Embodiment and Action

1 Quoted by Tracy, (1984), p. 55.
2 Quoted ibid., p. 47.
3 Swinburne (1977), pp. 103-4.
4 Jantzen (1984), p. 80.
5 Prestige (1936), p. 7; see Creel (1986) for an extensive discussion of the issues of divine impassibility.
6 See Polkinghorne (1988), ch. 4.
7 Vanstone (1982), p. 94 This reference is a warmer account of divine vulnerability than the coldy stoic account of Creel (1986), whose God is merely ignorant of the future choices of free agents and simply content that they should make their decisions for or against his will as they wish.
8 See, for example, Pagels (1985).
9 Jantzen (1984), p. 135.
10 See, for example, Pagels (1985), ch. 3.5.
11 Jantzen (1984), p. 142.
12 ibid., p. 136.
13 Peacocke (1979), p. 142.
14 Moltmann (1985), pp. 86-7.

15 Gunton (1978), p. 58.

16 Lovelock (1979).

17 For an account of the Einstein–Podolsky–Rosen experiment, see, for example, Polkinghorne (1984), ch. 7.

18 Hoyle (1960), in a work of fiction presents a picture of a thinking plasma.

19 Schrödinger (1944), pp. 92–3.

20 Barrow and Tipler (1986), p. 22 and ch. 7.

21 Macquarrie (1984), p. 49.

22 Peacocke (1986), p. 123.

23 Quoted, ibid., p. 22.

24 Polkinghorne (1988), ch. 5.

25 See, for example, Polkinghorne (1979), ch. 5.

26 Moltmann (1985), ch. 7.

27 Popper (1972), chs. 3 and 4.

28 Pollard (1958).

29 Bartholomew (1984), ch. 4.

30 Not all agree; see Eccles, J. C., Proc. Roy. Soc. *B227*, 411 (1986).

31 A comparison with quantum theory is instructive. Heisenberg's analysis of thought experiments only showed epistemological uncertainty (see Polkinghorne (1984), ch.5) but the conventional interpretation of the theory goes on to assert an ontological uncertainty (in contrast to the hidden variable version).

32 There may be connections here with the problems of quantum measurement; see Davies (1987), pp. 172–4.

33 Peacocke (1986), p. 28.

34 Prigogine and Stengers (1984), Polkinghorne (1988), ch. 3, Davies (1987).

35 Prigogine and Stengers (1984), p. 16.

36 ibid., p. 300.

37 Taylor (1972), p. 28.

38 Wiles (1986), p. 100.

39 Prigogine (1980).

Chapter 3 Providence

1 Newbigin (1986), pp. 39–40.

2 ibid, p. 67; cf. Capra (1975).

3 White (1985), p. 177.

4 Repeated seven times in Gen. 1.
5 Barrow and Tipler (1986).
6 Montefiore (1985), p. 161.
7 Dawkins (1986), p. 317.
8 Barrow and Tipler (1986), p. 11.
9 ibid., p. 124.
10 Bartholomew (1984), ch. 4.
11 Prigogine and Stengers (1984), chs. 5 and 6.
12 Monod (1972), p. 110.
13 Quoted in White (1985), p. 66.
14 Barbour (1966), p. 417.
15 Matt. 5.45.
16 Baelz (1968), p. 125.
17 Dawkins (1986), p. 126.
18 Baelz (1968), p. 126.
19 White (1985), p. 69.
20 Bartholomew (1984), p. 143.
21 Ramsey (1973), p. 21.
22 ibid., p. 22.
23 Farrer (1967), p. 68.
24 ibid.
25 Acts 4.30.
26 Rev. 19.6 (AV).
27 Quoted in Wiles (1986), p. 40.
28 Farrer (1967), p. 62.
29 Wiles (1986), p. 83.
30 ibid., p. 81.

Chapter 4   Miracle

1 Lewis (1947), p. 15.
2 Swinburne (1970), p. 1.
3 Farmer (1935), p. 108.
4 ibid., p. 110.
5 Jer. 24.
6 Quoted in Mascall (1956), p. 180.
7 Polkinghorne (1983), p. 79.

8   In Moule (1965), p. 25.

9   John 2.1-11.

10 1 Cor. 15.20.

11 Lewis (1947), p. 162.

12 Wisd. 19.18.

13 Farmer (1935), pp. 125-6.

14 Mark 4. 35-41, par.

15 Storr (1983), p. 339.

16 Matt. 11.2-6, par.

17 Acts 2.24, 36.

18 Swinburne (1981), p. 186.

19 Farmer (1935), p. 125.

20 Mark 6.5-6, par.

21 Augustine, *The City of God*, XXII, 8.

22 Lewis (1947), p. 201.

23 Polkinghorne (1983), ch. 8.

24 D. Hume, *An Enquiry Concerning Human Understanding*, X, from which the quotations which follow are also drawn.

25 *The Quarterly Review of the Churches' Fellowship for Psychical and Spiritual Study*, no. 125, p. 19 (1985).

26 Sanders (1985), p. 182.

27 Gen. 16.1-8.

28 Luke 1.18-20.

29 John 20. 24-9.

30 Matt 28.17.

31 Matt. 4.5-8.

32 Mark 8.11-12, par.

33 Matt. 11.2-6; Matt. 12.27-8 are exceptions in the synoptics.

34 Mark 16.6, par.; but cf. John 20.6-9.

35 Swinburne (1977), p. 192.

36 Quoted in Swinburne (1970), p. 69.

37 In Moule (1965), p. 42.

38 ibid., p. 14.

Chapter 5   Evil

1   Quoted in Hick (1966), p. 5n.

2   Ps. 73.3, 138.

3   1 Pet. 4.12, 13.
4   Isa. 11.9.
5   Rev. 21.4.
6   Ps. 44.23.
7   Isa. 45.7.
8   Baelz (1968), p. 64.
9   Job 38.2.
10 Storr (1983), p. 313.
11 ibid., p. 317.
12 Augustine, *Confessions*, VII, 5.
13 Augustine, *The City of God*, XI, 9.
14 Berger (1969), pp. 73–4.
15 Baelz (1968), p. 129.
16 Jantzen (1984), pp. 91–2.
17 Hick (1966), pp. 182, 280.
18 Quoted in Surin (1986), p. 95.
19 F. Dostoevsky, *The Brothers Karamazov*, ch. 5.4.
20 Augustine, *Enchiridion*, XXVII.
21 Rev. 7.10.
22 Creel (1986), p. 150.
23 ibid., p. 151.
24 Traditionally theologians have considered a third form, metaphysical evil, corresponding to the limitations inherent in finite beings. The traditional answer lay in the principle of plenitude – that it is good to have a great variety of beings, not all of which can enjoy maximal capacities. A world with beasts and men is better than a world with men only. In modern understanding the gradation of being is necessary if the God of love is the one who acts through the outworking of evolutionary process.
25 Hick (1966), pp. 303–13.
26 ibid., p. 308.
27 Polkinghorne (1988), p. 49.
28 Vanstone (1977), p. 62.
29 ibid., p. 63.
30 Farrer (1966), p. 87.
31 Lucas (1976), p. 29.
32 ibid., p. 30.
33 Julian of Norwich, *Revelations of Divine Love*, 27.
34 Col. 1.19–20.

Chapter 6   Prayer

1 Baelz (1968), p. 10.
2 Matt. 7.7, par.
3 Quoted in Brümmer (1984), p. 45.
4 Quoted, ibid., p. 25.
5 Luke 1.38.
6 Baelz (1968), p. 118.
7 Brümmer (1984), p. 54.
8 Lucas (1976), p. 40.
9 Mark 10.51, par.
10 Brümmer (1984), p. 54.
11 McDonald (1986), pp. 115–16.
12 Quoted in Brümmer (1984), p. 41.
13 Steinberg (1947), p. 120.
14 Baelz (1968), p. 35.
15 Gunstone (1986), p. 16.
16 Baelz (1968), p. 114.
17 1 Cor. 4.9.

Chapter 7   Time

1 Boethius, *On the Consolation of Philosophy*, 5.6.
2 Quoted in Prigogine and Stengers (1984), p. 294.
3 See, for example, Polkinghorne (1984), especially, chs. 6 and 8.
4 Prigogine and Stengers (1984), p. 16.
5 Swinburne (1977), p. 175.
6 Jer. 33.10–16.
7 Isa. 42.9.
8 Gen. 18.
9 Quoted in Gunton (1978), p. 180.
10 ibid., pp. 12f.
11 Quoted, ibid., p. 27.
12 Baelz (1968), p. 138.
13 Gunton (1978), p. 33.
14 Quoted, ibid., p. 36.

15 See, for example, Polkinghorne (1988), ch. 3.

16 Ward (1982).

17 ibid., p. 171.

18 Farrer (1967), p. 95.

19 Gunton (1978), p. 223.

20 Isa. 57.15.

21 Gunton (1978), p. 62.

22 Cobb and Griffin (1976).

23 Farrer (1967), p. 159.

24 White (1985), p. 131.

25 Vanstone (1982), p. 96.

26 Wiles (1986), pp. 37–8.

Chapter 8   Incarnation and Sacrament

1 Polkinghorne (1988), ch. 5.

2 Wiles (1986), p. 84.

3 Brown (1985), p. 236.

4 Wiles (1986), p. 89.

5 2 Cor. 5.17.

6 Polkinghorne (1988), ch. 6.

7 ibid., p. 80.

8 For a survey and critique of such models, see Brown (1985), ch. 5.

9 ibid., p. 231.

10 Baker (1970), p. 320.

11 Quoted in Brown (1985), p. 233.

12 See especially, Moltmann (1981).

13 ibid., p. 80.

14 ibid., p. 94 (my italics).

15 Wiles (1986), p. 90.

16 1 Cor. 15.44.

17 1 Cor. 15.37,42.

18 2 Cor. 5.1.

19 2 Cor. 5.2–3; see Barrett (1971), *ad loc.*

20 1 Cor. 15.50.

21 Rom. 12.4–8; 1 Cor. 12.12–31; see Robinson (1952).

22 Ignatius of Antioch, *Epistle to the Ephesians*, 20.

23 Thurian (1981).
24 The appeal to sacramental intuition has been popular among writers on science and theology; for example, Peacocke (1979), pp. 290–1; (1986), ch. 9; Polkinghorne (1986), ch. 7.
25 *ARCIC – The Final Report* (1982), CTS/SPCK, p. 21.
26 ibid., p. 22.
27 Col. 3.11.
28 O'Collins (1987), p. 156.

Chapter 9   Hope
1 Barrow and Tipler (1986), section 10.6.
2 ibid., p. 659.
3 2 Cor. 5.4.
4 Rom. 8.21.
5 2 Cor. 5.17.
6 Vanstone (1977), p. 66.
7 Peacocke (1986), p. 98.
8 Bartholomew (1984), ch. 4.
9 Geach (1977), p. 58.
10 Lucas (1976), p. 30.
11 Rom. 11.15.

Bibliography

Baelz; P. (1968) *Prayer and Providence*, SCM Press

Baker, J. A. (1970) *The Foolishness of God*, Darton, Longman and Todd

Barbour, I. G. (1966) *Issues in Science and Religion*, SCM Press

Barrett, C. K. (1971) *The First Epistle to the Corinthians*, A. & C. Black

Barrow, J. D., and Tipler, F. J. (1986) *The Anthropic Cosmological Principle*, Oxford University Press

Bartholomew, D. J. (1984) *God of Chance*, SCM Press

Berger, P. (1969) *A Rumour of Angels*, Penguin

Brown, D. (1985) *The Divine Trinity*, Duckworth

Brümmer, V. (1984) *What Are We Doing When We Pray?*, SCM Press

Bryant, C. (1983) *Jung and the Christian Way*, Darton, Longman and Todd

Capra, F. (1975) *The Tao of Physics*, Wildwood House

Cobb, J. B., and Griffin, D. R. (1976) *Process Theology, An Introductory Exposition*, Westminster

Creel, R. E. (1986) *Divine Impassibility*, Cambridge University Press

Davies, P. (1983) *God and the New Physics*, Dent

– (1987) *The Cosmic Blueprint*, Heinemann

Dawkins, R. (1986) *The Blind Watchmaker*, Longman

Dukas, H., and Hoffman, B. (1979) *Albert Einstein, the Human Side*, Princeton University Press

Farmer, H. H. (1935) *The World and God*, Nisbet

Farrer, A. (1966) *A Science of God?*, Geoffrey Bles

– (1967) *Faith and Speculation*, A. & C. Black

Gardner, M. (1983) *The Whys of a Philosophical Scrivener*, Oxford University Press

Geach, P. T. (1977) *Providence and Evil*, Cambridge University Press

Gunstone, J. (1986) *The Lord is Our Healer*, Hodder and Stoughton

Gunton, C. E. (1978) *Being and Becoming*, Oxford University Press

Hick, J. (1966) *Evil and the God of Love*, Macmillan

Hooykaas, H. (1972) *Religion and the Rise of Modern Science*, Scottish Academic Press

Hoyle, F. (1960) *The Black Cloud*, Heinemann

– (1983) *The Intelligent Universe*, Michael Joseph

Jantzen, G. (1984) *God's World, God's Body*, Darton, Longman and Todd
Kasper, W. (1984) E. T.: *The God of Jesus Christ*, SCM Press
Lewis, C. S. (1947) *Miracles*, Geoffrey Bles
Lovelock, J. E. (1979) *Gaia*, Oxford University Press
Lucas, J. R. (1976) *Freedom and Grace*, SPCK
Macquarrie, J. (1984) *In Search of Deity*, SCM Press
McDonald, H. D. (1986) *The God Who Responds*, James Clarke
Mascall, E. L. (1956) *Christian Theology and Natural Science*, Longman
Moltmann, J. (1981) E. T.: *The Trinity and the Kingdom of God*, SCM Press
- (1985) E. T.: *God in Creation*, SCM Press
Monod, J. (1972) E. T.: *Chance and Necessity*, Collins
Montefiore, H. (1985) *The Probability of God*, SCM Press
Moule, C. F. D. (ed.) (1965) *Miracles*, Mowbray
Newbigin, L. (1986) *Foolishness to the Greeks*, SPCK
O'Collins, G. (1987) *Jesus Risen*, Darton, Longman and Todd
Pagels, H. (1985) *Perfect Symmetry*, Michael Joseph
Pailin, D. A. (1986) *Groundwork of Philosophy of Religion*, Epworth
Peacocke, A. R. (1979) *Creation and the World of Science*, Oxford University Press
- (1986) *God and the New Biology*, Dent
Polkinghorne, J. C. (1979) *The Particle Play*, W. H. Freeman
- (1983) *The Way the World Is*, Triangle
- (1984) *The Quantum World*, Longman
- (1986) *One World*, SPCK
- (1988) *Science and Creation*, SPCK
Pollard, W. G. (1958) *Chance and Providence*, Faber
Popper, K. (1972) *Objective Knowledge*, Oxford University Press
Prestige, G. L. (1936) *God in Patristic Thought*, SPCK
Prigogine, I. (1980) *From Being to Becoming*, W. H. Freeman
Prigogine, I., and Stengers, I. (1984) *Order out of Chaos*, Heinemann
Ramsey, I. T. (1973) *Models for Divine Activity*, SCM Press
Robinson, J. A. T. (1952) *The Body*, SCM Press
Russell, C. A. (1985) *Cross Currents*, IVP
Sanders, E. P. (1985) *Jesus and Judaism*, SCM Press
Schrödinger, E. (1944) *What is Life?*, Cambridge University Press
Steinberg, M. (1947) *Basic Judaism*, Harcourt, Brace and World
Storr, A. (ed.) (1983) *Jung – Selected Writings*, Fontana
Surin, K. (1986) *Theology and the Problem of Evil*, Blackwell
Swinburne, R. (1970) *The Concept of Miracle*, Macmillan
- (1977) *The Coherence of Theism*, Oxford University Press

110

BIBLIOGRAPHY

– (1981) *Faith and Reason*, Oxford University Press

Taylor, J. V. (1972) *The Go-Between God*, SCM Press

Thurian, M. (1981) *The Mystery of the Eucharist*, Mowbray

Tracy, T. F. (1984) *God, Action and Embodiment*, Eerdmans

Vanstone, W. H. (1977) *Love's Endeavour, Love's Expense*, Darton, Longman and Todd

– (1982) *The Stature of Waiting*, Darton, Longman and Todd

Ward, K. (1982) *Rational Theology and the Creativity of God*, Blackwell

White, V. (1985) *The Fall of a Sparrow*, Paternoster Press

Wiles, M. F. (1986) *God's Action in the World*, SCM Press

Index

accelerated naturalism 47-8
action, divine 2, 5-7, 10-17, 21, 23, 25-7, 31-5, 36-8, 44, 46, 52-3, 68, 84, 98-9
anthropic principle 3, 24, 37, 39-40, 95-6
Aquinas, St Thomas 20, 77, 83
ARCIC 93
Augustine, St 47, 61, 69-70, 93-4
Auschwitz 7-8

Baelz, P. 10, 41, 60, 62, 69, 74-5, 80
Baker, J.A. 87
Barbour, I.G. 40-1
Barrow, J.D. 39-40, 95-6
Barth, K. 79-80
Bartholomew, D. 40-1, 97
Berger, P. 61-2
best possible world 64
bifurcation 32
Boethius 77
Brown, D. 7, 86-7
Brümmer, V. 7, 71
Bryant, C. 9
Bultmann, R. 11

chance and necessity 38-40
coincidence 48-9
complementary metaphysic 2, 26, 33, 85, 87
creationism 39
Creel, R. 64
cross of Christ 68

Davies, P.C.W. 6
Dawkins, R. 39, 41
deism 1-2, 5-6, 36, 38, 41, 79, 99
depth psychology 9
Descartes, R. 18
dipolar God 3, 80-1, 87-8
Dostoevsky, F. 63-4
double agency 11-12
dualism, Cartesian 18
dynamical systems 2, 28-30, 32, 78-9

Eastern religions 24, 36
economy, divine 8
Einstein, A. 4, 15, 77-8
embodiment, divine 2, 15, 18-23, 32, 34, 62-3
energy 13, 32
Epicurus 59
evil 3, 17, 59-68
existentialism 10-11

Farmer, H.H. 45, 48, 52
Farrer, A.M. 11-13, 42-3, 67, 83
fideism 10-11
free process defence 66-7
free will defence 65-6
freedom 2-3, 6, 10, 23, 30, 33-4, 67, 70

Gaia hypothesis 23
Galton, F. 75
Gardner, M. 10-11
Geach, P.T. 98